To Rosie.
For Everything.

BAKING WITH A HEALTHY TWIST

Nourish
CAKES

MARIANNE STEWART

Foreword by Dr Rebecca Hiscutt PhD, Founder of Relish Wellbeing
Photography by Catherine Frawley

quadrille

Publishing Director Sarah Lavelle
Project Editor Kathy Steer
Editor Harriet Webster
Creative Director Helen Lewis
Designer Gemma Hayden
Photographer Catherine Frawley
Props Stylists Catherine and Michael Frawley
Food Stylist Marianne Stewart
Nutrition Consultant Dr Rebecca Hiscutt
Production Director Vincent Smith
Production Controller Tom Moore

Published in 2018 by Quadrille, an imprint of
Hardie Grant Publishing

Quadrille
52–54 Southwark Street
London SE1 1UN
quadrille.com

Text © Marianne Stewart 2018
Design and Photography © Quadrille 2018

ISBN 978 178713 116 3

Printed in China

Notes on the recipes

WF = wheat-free
GF = gluten-free
DF = dairy-free
VG = vegan

Ingredients are listed in UK metric followed by
US imperial/cup measurements. Please follow
one system of measurement when following
the recipes.

Eggs are medium unless specified otherwise.

Salt is Maldon sea salt unless specified otherwise.

Lemons and limes should be unwaxed.

I prefer to use Dove's Farm rice flour but find
a brand you like.

The publisher wishes to thank the following for their
generous loans of props and equipment for this book:

The Linen Works (www.thelinenworks.co.uk)
KitchenAid (kitchenaid.com)
Microplane (microplaneintl.com)
Kitchens Cookshop, Bristol (steamer.co.uk)
Toby Gamston (tobiasgeorge.com)
WAB Home (wabhome.co.uk)

Contents

6   Foreword

7   Introduction

8   Baking Basics

10 Light & Zesty

38 Vibrant & Fruity

66 Warm & Nutty

102 Dark & Spicy

130 Basic Recipes

136 Ingredient Index

138 Index

142 Free-From Index

144 Acknowledgements

Foreword by Dr Rebecca Hiscutt

NOURISH CAKES BRING US A SCRUMPTIOUS COLLECTION OF CAKES, SHOWING HOW WE CAN ENJOY THE DELICIOUSNESS OF FOOD WHILE ALSO NOURISHING OUR BODIES.

Marianne and I share the same love and passion for good food based on real ingredients that have been grown or produced with love and care. This beautiful book encourages readers to discover new ingredients and nourish their bodies while making amazing cakes to share with family and friends.

Food has such an impact on our everyday lives. It affects our energy levels and influences our mood and health. As a nutrition consultant I spend every day helping people to utilize the power of food to feel as good as they possibly can, and to love everything they eat. **Nourish Cakes** encourages you to eat nutrient-packed, wholesome food while enjoying the whole experience.

Imagine enjoying a Salted Caramel & Chocolate Tart (see page 115) that you know contains rich dark chocolate packed with antioxidants to give you a mood boost. Or enjoying a chocolate brownie without the sluggish feeling that often follows. A traditional brownie contains sugar and white flour that is quickly absorbed, causing blood sugar levels to rise quickly, leading to tiredness. Adding foods rich in fibre and protein can slow the absorption of sugar so these spikes in blood sugar levels are reduced – the Pecan-studded Sweet Potato Brownie recipe on page 68 does this beautifully! This means blood sugar levels remain far more stable after eating a treat.

Eating a variety of natural unprocessed foods is the best way to optimize your health and well-being. I love the diversity of the ingredients used in the recipes in this book, with an array of vegetables, fruit and spices, as well as nuts and seeds. The Heritage Carrot Layer Cake (see page 73) uses three different varieties of carrot, all of which are rich in different health-promoting plant compounds.

In **Nourish Cakes** you will find recipes to suit all dietary needs and preferences, so everyone has the chance to enjoy a piece of cake whether they are gluten-free, vegan, or if you simply enjoy good food! How wonderful that you can bake a cake to share with everyone, no matter what their allergies or intolerances.

Baking can be a wonderful way to focus the mind and get lost in the art of making a cake. I find it incredibly relaxing and love making cakes and nourishing sweet treats for my family and friends. **Nourish Cakes** will have a permanent position on my cake stand as I work my way through the recipes to make cakes for lunchboxes, to give to bake sales, to bring out proudly after a meal or simply to have on hand to share with friends who pop in. I'm constantly asked for ideas for puddings or alternatives to the (less nourishing) snacks and cakes available everywhere, so now I can recommend a book jam-packed with delicious cakes to nourish both the body and the soul.

Thank you for giving us cakes we can enjoy together, Marianne.

Happy eating and baking!

Introduction

Food is a necessity, as we need it to nourish and nurture our bodies, but treating ourselves shouldn't mean leaving our bodies feeling sick and sluggish. **Say goodbye to guilt!**

This cookery book is a celebrated collection of good quality ingredients that will leave you feeling healthy and energetic. A true discovery of new and exciting 'free-from' ingredients, taming them to behave in a way that works wonders in the kitchen. The focus is on all those amazing things you can eat that make you feel alive. **It's about baking your cake and eating it too.**

I became a cake-maker because I have always loved treats. When I was a child one of my favourite games to play with my step-grandfather and sister Rosie was 'Hunt the Peppermint and the Coin'. Rosie would hunt for the coin and, you guessed it, I would hunt for the peppermint. Years later she became an accountant, and I became a pastry chef!

In my heart of hearts, I'm really a cake geek. As a priority, treats from my own oven must always taste good, but **I no longer believe that to taste good they have to be filled with 'bad-for-you' ingredients**. I love figuring out new ways to create great flavour and texture using nourishing ingredients. Fresh fruit and vegetables add moisture and texture in gluten-free bakes, nuts and nut butters help replace dairy-based fats. Ingredients like flaxseed play a structural role, and deliver essential fatty acids that are good for brain and heart health. And the highly celebrated coconut in all its forms is super-useful for adding creamy richness and texture and is packed with health-promoting nutrients.

I relish my time working with a variety of ingredients that creatively bring a wider set of flavours and nutrients to the tables of my friends and family. These ingredients now make it possible to share my baking with everyone, no matter what their food intolerances.

As a final note, many of the recipes in this book have been crafted in small quantities. The whole cakes are perfect for small to medium gatherings, while the individual treats are easily divided over afternoon tea or in the office. With these portions, I aim to encourage balance and allow your treat to feel truly special – and make sure there's still enough for sharing.

Welcome to a new approach to baking and creating some delicious sweet treats (not **just** cakes) for yourself, your friends and your family in your own kitchen. **Cake is still cake, and you don't want to eat it at every meal, but you can bake better, smarter and more inventively.**

Long live cake!

Marianne xx

Baking Basics

Make sure you read through the whole recipe, so you know how much time you need and what equipment to have ready. It sounds simple, but most baking requires a little planning, so looking ahead helps make the whole process easier.

Prepare everything you need before you start baking. Chefs call this 'mis-en-place' – basically getting organized. It may seem like preparing and weighing all your ingredients in one go takes a while, but it also means you can then concentrate on putting the recipe together. This is important when you are making a cake for the first time.

Weigh out your ingredients carefully. I use digital scales for accuracy, and proper measuring spoons for salt, baking powder, etc. One teaspoon should be exactly 5ml and one tablespoon is 15ml (3 tsp). Tablespoon measurements can vary in different countries, so adjust if needed. Always level off your measuring spoons, rather than leaving the ingredient heaped. Throughout the book, I have used Maldon sea salt, which is flaky, so if you use fine sea salt you will need to reduce the quantities by approximately one-third.

Every oven is different. It is so important to understand that temperatures and timings given for these recipes are what have worked in my oven, and are just a starting point. You may find your cakes need to stay in a little longer, come out earlier or the temperature might just need adjusting, as you will have a different appliance. Keep an eye on your cakes when you are first baking them and make a note (yes, please do scribble on the book!) if you need to change anything. Also, be clear about whether you are using a fan or conventional oven, as the temperature settings are quite different.

Turn your cakes. Ovens often have hot spots, or if you are using more than one shelf in the oven then the top one will naturally be hotter. It is a good idea to move the cake tins around – either turn

them 180 degrees and/or swap the shelves over just over halfway through baking. Don't do this too early on in the baking time, or you risk the drop in temperature affecting the rise in your cakes. Only open the oven door when the cakes have already risen and are looking semi-set on top. This normally happens about half to two-thirds of the way through the baking time.

Be consistent with the brands you buy. This is the case for particular ingredients such as coconut cream, dairy-free yoghurt and the rice flour blend I use. I want to encourage experimenting and trying new ingredients, but changing to another brand may give you different results, so try to stick to what you know works.

GLUTEN-FREE BAKING

Each different flour has its own characteristics, but there are a few general rules to consider when going gluten-free. The most obvious thing to note is that you need to mimic the effects of gluten – the protein (or more accurately the collection of proteins) present in wheat and other flours, giving it stretch and extensibility. I have tried as much as possible to do this naturally with the recipes; increasing the protein content with a higher proportion of eggs, adding in ground flaxseed and even grated fruit and vegetables, which help hold the cake together. You can also use one of two gluten replacers: psyllium husk and xanthan gum. They work in a similar way, but xanthan gum is more effective with drier recipes such as pastry, whereas the psyllium works well in batters, such as for pancakes or breads. They are there to give recipes a structural boost where needed, but can be omitted if you don't have them.

Gluten-free flours generally require more hydration, so many of the cake batters will seem quite loose. This is crucial to prevent dryness after baking. The starches in the flours also require more time to hydrate, so it's important to rest the batter before baking. You may also find that you will need to bake these extra hydrated cake batters for longer than you would expect. Baking in smaller tins and separating out the mixture into several tins for layer cakes also works well for gluten-free cake batters, as it gives them better texture.

A lot of the recipes are much lower in fat content than conventional ones. Obviously this can be a good choice health-wise, but it is also because gluten-free flours do not absorb fats as effectively as wheat flour, so can easily become greasy with too much oil (or butter). In order to prevent dryness, I have included ground nuts, dairy-free yoghurt and flaxseed to add extra richness, and grated or puréed fruit and vegetables – a satisfyingly healthy way to replace fat!

EQUIPMENT

The most important piece of kitchen kit I can recommend for successful baking is a set of **digital kitchen scales**. Baking is a bit like a science experiment; but you don't want it to get too experimental! If everything is not weighed correctly, this can easily put the recipe out of balance and give you variable results.

I also have a beautiful heavy-duty **stand mixer**, which, as a professional baker, I use frequently. However, all the whisking required in these recipes can be accomplished with a good-quality **hand-held electric whisk**.

A **blender** is probably one of the more crucial bits of kit when it comes to grinding nuts, creamy fillings and tough sticky ingredients such as dates. If you want a machine that lasts and works well with the recipes in this book, as well as for smoothie-making, then I would recommend looking for the following features: high wattage motor (800w or higher); more than one size cup attachment for different quantities; two blade attachments – one for blending and one (flat blade) for grinding. I use the blender blade for anything creamy, liquid or sticky and the grinding attachment for grinding nuts or dry ingredients. You can also purchase a good-quality grinder separately for grinding nuts, spices or flours, if you prefer. They are not normally expensive, but buy one that has a large capacity so you don't have to grind in several batches.

A **food processor** can be useful for fine chopping, or even processing ingredients such as dates if you don't have a blender. As with most electrical appliances, I would recommend a machine that is durable but simple – too many extra functions normally just means something to go wrong.

For grating fruit and vegetables, I would recommend buying a flat **microplane zester**, which is used for finely grating citrus peel. These are best for removing just the outer part of the zest and helps you get the most flavour from the fruit. For coarse grating, use the large part of a **box grater** – the part of the grater you would use for hard cheese, and for finely grated vegetables use the grater setting one size smaller than this.

A decent set of **kitchen knives** is helpful for slicing and chopping; if I had to recommend just one knife it would be a chef's knife as I get the most use out of mine.

As a rule, I tend to use **sandwich tins** (shallow cake tins) for baking individual sponges that are then layered, and deeper **springform or loose-based tins** for cakes such as the Christmas fruit and root cake on page 121 or whole cheesecakes. Anodized aluminium is best for baking sponges, since it distributes the heat evenly, while darker coloured non-stick tins are best for pastry, as they brown better. Silicone moulds are fantastic for all shapes and sizes of small cakes – I rarely use them for larger cakes, though, as they do not hold their shape well. My favourites are oval friand moulds and mini bundt moulds, but you can find a whole range online, so do play around!

Light
+ ZESTY

These mini cheesecakes are beautifully tart and refreshing, and so pretty in their mini sizes. Making desserts in individual silicone moulds is a great way to keep the portion sizes moderate, while making them feel like an indulgent treat.

Blueberry & Lime Cheesecakes

WF | GF | DF | VG

MAKES 8 MINI CHEESECAKES

1 quantity of Cheesecake Base
  (see page 131)

FOR THE FILLING

100g (3½oz/generous ¾ cup)
  cashew nuts
pinch of salt
80g (3oz/scant ½ cup) coconut
  oil, melted
100g (3½oz/⅓ cup) brown rice
  syrup (vegan) or honey
finely grated zest of 3 limes
juice of 1½ limes (about 40g/
  1½fl oz/heaping 2½ tbsp)
200g (7oz/1½ cups) coconut cream
120g (4½oz/1 cup) fresh
  blueberries, plus extra to
  decorate

Make the Cheesecake Base according to the instructions on page 131, using an 8-hole oval silicone/financier mould (each about 7.5 x 5.5cm/3 x 2¼in).

For the filling, soak the cashews in cold water for 1 hour. Strain and blend in a blender or food processor with the salt until as fine as possible. Add the coconut oil and blend again until completely smooth. Add the syrup or honey, lime zest and juice and the coconut cream and blend again, until well mixed and smooth.

Fill the silicone moulds almost to the top, then top with the blueberries. Push down gently into the mixture. Chill in the fridge overnight before de-moulding and serving, or in the freezer for 2 or more hours. If frozen, they are easier to de-mould, but best left to soften in the fridge for an hour or two.

Decorate with blueberries. Keep in a covered container in the fridge for 2–3 days.

VARIATION:

Replace the lime juice with the same quantity of lemon juice and the zest with the finely grated zest of 2 lemons.

Lime, coconut and courgette (zucchini) has become a new classic, but not all cakes that appear in cafés are allergy-friendly or even that healthy. This recipe is tart, fresh and delicious, but still suitable for the gluten- and dairy-intolerant, as well as benefiting from the nutrient plus-points of extra fibre and protein from the nuts, rice flour and flaxseeds. Trust me though, you would never know!

Lime, Coconut & Courgette Cake

WF | GF | DF

MAKES A 20-CM (8-IN) CAKE
to serve 10–12

4 medium courgettes (zucchini), washed and grated
finely grated zest and juice of 6 limes (see below)
5 eggs
300g (10½oz/1⅔ cups) golden caster (granulated) sugar or demerara (raw brown) sugar
225g (7¾oz/1¾ cups) rice flour
100g (3½oz/1 cup) ground almonds
5 tsp ground flaxseed
1¼ tsp bicarbonate of soda (baking soda)
50g (1¾oz/⅔ cup) desiccated (dry unsweetened) coconut
coconut oil, for greasing

FOR THE LIME CURD
90g (3fl oz/6 tbsp) lime juice (left over from the cake recipe)
5 tsp cornflour (cornstarch) or tapioca flour
90g (3¼oz/½ cup) golden caster (granulated) sugar or demerara (raw brown) sugar
160g (5¾oz/½ cup) coconut cream
5 egg yolks
45g (1½oz/¼ cup) coconut oil

Layer the grated courgette between double thicknesses of kitchen paper or tea towels and press down to extract the juice. Set aside for 30 minutes, making sure the courgette is well drained. Weigh out 465g (1½lb), and add the lime zest and 4 tablespoons of the juice. Set aside the remaining juice for the curd.

Place the eggs in the bowl of a stand mixer, add the sugar and whisk on medium-high speed for 5 minutes, or until pale and doubled in volume. Alternatively use an electric hand whisk.

Fold the courgette through the egg mixture until well incorporated. Sift together the rice flour, ground almonds, flaxseed and bicarbonate of soda. Add the coconut and fold this mixture through the cake batter. Leave to rest for 10 minutes.

Preheat the oven to 180°C/fan 160°C/350°F. Grease 2 x 20-cm (8-in) round cake tins, at least 5cm (2in) deep, with coconut oil and line with baking parchment. Divide the cake batter evenly between the tins and bake for 40 minutes, or until browned and the tops spring back when gently pressed. Cool the cakes in their tins on a wire rack until just warm, then remove from the tins and cool on the rack until cold. Chill thoroughly before slicing and filling.

For the curd, add a little of the lime juice to the cornflour in a bowl to make a loose paste. Place the remaining juice, along with half of the sugar and the coconut cream, in a small pan and heat gently to simmering point, stirring. Add the cornflour paste and cook for 4–5 minutes, until the mixture has thickened and has lost its floury taste.

Whisk the remaining sugar with the egg yolks. Add a little of the hot mixture from the pan to the eggs and mix well, then pour back into the pan. Place

ingredients and method continue overleaf

TO DECORATE

500g (1lb 2oz/1⅔ cups) coconut
  cream, chilled
coconut flakes, freshly grated lime
  zest and edible flowers

over a very low heat and cook for
3–4 minutes until the mix has
thickened. Mix in the coconut
oil. Scrape into a bowl, cover and
chill until firm and cold.

To assemble the cake, slice each
layer in half and, if the tops are
uneven, trim these as well with a
long serrated knife.

Whisk 150g (5¼oz/½ cup) of
the lime curd with the coconut
cream. Place the first layer of
cake on a serving plate and
spread evenly with half of the
remaining curd. Place the next
cake layer on top and spread
with half of the lime-coconut
cream. Place the next cake layer
on top and spread with the
remaining curd. The final layer
of cake should be one of the
bottom halves of the cake; place
this crust side up. Spoon on the
remaining lime cream. Decorate
with coconut flakes, grated lime
zest and edible flowers.

TIP:

*Make sure the courgettes are firm, and not too large. Too much
softness or too many seeds in the centre can affect the cake's texture.*

When my sister requested a gluten-free, dairy-free lemon meringue pie that tasted really good, I knew this wouldn't be the quickest recipe-testing task! I managed to problem-solve one step further, and make it vegan-friendly too. They bake easiest in smaller tart tins, and although there are quite a few steps to this recipe, both the pastry making and baking can be done in advance.

Lemon Meringue Pies

WF | GF | DF | VG

MAKES 5 SMALL PIES

1 quantity of Pastry (see page 130)
Candied lemon strips (see page 133), to decorate

FOR THE FILLING

finely grated zest and juice of 2 lemons (about 165g/5½fl oz/ ¾ cup juice)
30g (1oz/¼ cup) cornflour (cornstarch)
large pinch of sea salt
150g (5¼oz/generous ¾ cup) golden caster (granulated) sugar or demerara (raw brown) sugar
150g (5fl oz/⅔ cup) orange juice
2½ tsp agar agar
15g (½oz/1 tbsp) coconut oil
180g (6½oz) firm silken tofu
½ tsp ground turmeric (optional)

FOR THE VEGAN MERINGUE

800g (1lb 12oz/3 cups) canned chickpeas in water, not brine
½ tsp lemon juice
190g (6¾oz/1 cup) golden caster (granulated) sugar or demerara (raw brown) sugar, ground until fine
¼ tsp xanthan gum (optional)

Make the pastry according to the instructions on page 130, using it to line 5 x 10-cm (4-in) individual tart tins.

Preheat the oven to 200°C/fan 180°C/400°F and put a baking sheet in the oven to heat. Line the base of the pastry cases with baking parchment, then fill with rice or lentils. Bake on the tray for 20 minutes, or until the edges of the pastry are just beginning to brown. Remove the parchment and rice and cook the pastry cases for a further 3–4 minutes, or until the bases look dry (this is 'blind baking'). Cool in the tins on a wire rack. Reduce the oven to 170°C/fan 150°C/340°F.

For the filling, mix 1 tablespoon of the lemon juice with the cornflour (cornstarch) in a bowl to form a paste, and set aside.

Add the remaining lemon juice and all the zest, along with the salt, sugar, orange juice and agar agar to a pan and bring gently to the boil, stirring. Once the mixture starts to boil, add the cornflour paste and stir thoroughly. Simmer, stirring for 5 minutes, or until thickened. Add the coconut oil and stir through.

Pulse the tofu in a food processor until smooth. Add the cooked lemon mixture and turmeric, if using, and pulse again to mix well. Divide this mixture between the pastry cases, filling them as close to the top as possible.

Bake the tarts for 15 minutes, or until just starting to puff up. They should still have a little wobble, but will firm up when cooled. Cool on a wire rack, then remove from the tins before completely cold. Chill for a few hours before topping with the baked meringues.

For the meringue, strain the liquid from the chickpeas into a pan. Bring to a simmer over a

method continues overleaf

medium-low heat, and cook until the liquid has reduced to 135g (4¾fl oz/½ cup), roughly by half. Set aside to cool.

Preheat the oven to 120°C/fan 100°C/250°F. Using a marker pen, trace circles around a tart tin on a sheet of baking parchment, to make 5 guide shapes for your meringues. Flip the paper over and place on a baking sheet.

Whisk the cooled chickpea liquid for 5–10 minutes until it becomes light and fluffy and looks like whisked egg whites. This will take much longer than with normal egg whites, so be patient!

Once the chickpea liquid holds soft peaks, add the lemon juice and sprinkle over one-quarter of the sugar. Whisk until this dissolves into the mixture, about 1 minute, then add the next quarter. Whisk again and add the remaining sugar in the same way, whisking well in between. Whisk until the meringue feels smooth to the touch, with no grains of sugar. Add the xanthan gum, if using, whisking in well.

Either pipe or spoon the meringue onto the circles on the baking parchment, keeping inside the circle; they should be slightly smaller so that they sit neatly on top of the tarts. Bake for 10 minutes, then reduce the oven temperature to 100°C/fan 80°C/210°F and cook for another hour, or until the outside is crisp and holds its shape well and the inside is still soft.

Let the meringues cool, then lift them gently off the paper and place on top of the filled lemon tarts. This is best done no more than a few hours before serving, so the meringue does not become soggy. Decorate with candied lemon strips.

TIP:
If you just want a lemon tart, omit the meringue stage and serve with a little crème fraîche instead.

This recipe is incredibly versatile and surprisingly simple to make. You can prepare the mix in advance and keep it unbaked in the fridge. They look beautiful undecorated, or simply finished with glacé icing. For a special occasion, jazz it up with the dairy-free cream topping and rhubarb twists!

Rhubarb & Orange Bundt Cakes

WF | GF | DF

MAKES 12 CAKES

Candied Rhubarb Twists (see page 135), to decorate

100g orange segments, cut into chunks and pips removed
200g (7oz) rhubarb, topped and tailed and cut into pieces
135g (4¾oz/¾ cup) golden caster (granulated) sugar
3 eggs
135g (4¾oz/1⅓ cups) ground almonds
1½ tsp tapioca flour or cornflour (cornstarch)
2 tsp rice flour
scant ½ tsp bicarbonate of soda (baking soda)
coconut oil, for greasing

FOR THE RHUBARB & ORANGE CREAM (OPTIONAL)

200g (7oz/¾ cup) coconut cream, chilled
50g (1¾oz) leftover rhubarb and orange purée
20g (¾oz/1½ tbsp) coconut oil, melted and cooled
20g (¾oz/2¼ tbsp) golden icing (confectioners') sugar or caster (superfine) sugar

Place the orange pieces in a pan and cover with 150g (5fl oz/⅔ cup) water. Cover and cook over a medium heat for 30 minutes, or until just soft. If the water runs low, top it up. Add the rhubarb, cover and cook for another 5 minutes. Uncover and simmer until 1 tablespoon of liquid remains.

Cool, then purée the fruit mix in a blender. Weigh out 185g (6½oz) into a bowl, keeping any leftover for later, then stir in the sugar with a balloon whisk. Add the eggs and whisk until smooth. Sift together the ground almonds, flours and bicarbonate of soda (baking soda) and whisk this into the mixture. It should be quite loose, but not aerated.

Preheat the oven to 170ºC/fan 150ºC/340ºF and grease

2 x 6-hole individual silicone bundt moulds, about 7cm (2¾in) across, with coconut oil. Place the moulds on a baking sheet and fill to just below the top with the cake batter. Bake for 40 minutes, or until well browned and they spring back when pressed.

Cool the cakes slightly in the moulds, then tip the whole mould upside down to remove. Cool on a wire rack until completely cold, then chill in a covered container.

If making the rhubarb and orange cream, gently whisk together all the ingredients until well blended and thick. Do not overwhisk. Chill for 30 minutes, then spoon or pipe on top of the cakes and decorate with rhubarb twists.

VARIATION:
Top with a little glacé icing by mixing some of the leftover purée with some icing (confectioners') sugar to create a thick glaze.

This recipe is a twist on the classic lemon loaf cake, updated to include one of my favourite teas, Earl Grey. When I was living in Paris, I fell in love with the Mariage Frères teas. My favourite was their Earl Grey French Blue, into which they add dried blue cornflowers. It seemed only appropriate, therefore, to add some edible blue cornflowers to the decoration!

Lemon & Earl Grey Loaf Cakes

WF | GF | DF

MAKES 6 CAKES

1 Earl Grey tea bag (or 1 tsp loose leaf Earl Grey tea)
120g (4¼oz/⅔ cup) golden caster (granulated) sugar or demerara (raw brown) sugar
½ yellow courgette (zucchini), grated
¼ swede (rutabaga), peeled and grated
15g (½fl oz/1 tbsp) lemon juice
finely grated zest of 2 lemons
2 eggs
40g (1½fl oz/heaping 2½ tbsp) rapeseed (canola) oil
75g (2¾oz/¾ cup) ground almonds
90g (3¼oz/¾ cup) rice flour
1½ tsp baking powder
¼ tsp bicarbonate of soda (baking soda)
¼ tsp xanthan gum (optional)
coconut oil, for greasing

FOR THE EARL GREY ICING

120g (4¼oz/¾ cup plus 2 tbsp) golden icing (confectioners') sugar
juice of ¼ lemon
25g (1fl oz/2 tbsp) strongly brewed Earl Grey tea
1 tsp loose Earl Grey tea (from tea bags or loose leaf)
blue cornflowers (optional)

Empty the contents of the tea bag into a bowl with the sugar, cover and infuse for a few hours or overnight if possible. Then grind in a blender until fine.

Place the courgette (zucchini) between some kitchen paper to drain off the excess moisture. Place 80g (3oz) swede (rutabaga) and 80g (3oz) of the courgette into a bowl and sprinkle over the lemon juice and zest. Set aside.

In a bowl, whisk together the eggs, sugar and oil for 5 minutes, or until pale and slightly thickened. Fold in the grated vegetables. Sift together the ground almonds, flour, raising agents and xanthan gum, if using. Fold into the cake mixture gently, until it is lump-free. Leave for 10 minutes.

Preheat the oven to 180°C/fan 160°C/350°F. Grease 6 mini loaf tins, about 9 x 6cm (3½ x 2½in), with coconut oil and line with baking parchment or disposable loaf cases.

Fill the tins almost to the top with the mixture and bake in the top half of the oven for 30 minutes, or until the tops spring back and an inserted cocktail stick comes out clean.

Cool the cakes in the tins until just warm, then turn out onto a wire rack to cool completely. For disposable cases, just cool in the cases.

For the icing, sift the icing (confectioners') sugar into a bowl and add the lemon juice and enough tea to form an icing the thickness of double (heavy) cream. Pour the icing over the cooled cakes, and top with a little sprinkle of tea leaves and blue cornflowers, if you have them.

Rhubarb and custard is a classic combination, and the orange buckwheat pastry pairs perfectly with both. All the elements can be made separately and assembled on the day of serving, making this a great make-ahead dessert.

Rhubarb & Custard Tart

WF | GF | DF | VG

MAKES 5 SMALL TARTS

1 quantity of Vegan Pastry Cream (see page 131)
Candied Orange Strips (see page 133), to decorate (optional)

FOR THE PASTRY

2 tsp gram (chickpea) flour
2 tsp ground flaxseed
70g (2½oz//⅓ cup) coconut cream
45g (1½oz/¼ cup) coconut oil
1 tsp cider vinegar
finely grated zest of 1 orange
100g (3½oz/generous ¾ cup) buckwheat flour
40g (1½oz/⅓ cup) rice flour
60g (2¼oz/⅔ cup) ground almonds
60g (2¼oz/5 tbsp) rapadura or light muscovado (soft brown) sugar
large pinch of sea salt
¼ tsp xanthan gum (optional)

FOR THE POACHED RHUBARB

200g (7fl oz/scant 1 cup) orange juice
200g (7oz/1 cup) golden caster (granulated) sugar or demerara (raw brown) sugar
400g (14oz) tender, pink rhubarb, trimmed and cut into pieces roughly 5 x 1 x ½cm (2 x ½ x ¼in) long

For the pastry, whisk together the gram flour, flaxseed, coconut cream, oil, cider vinegar and orange zest in a bowl until well blended. Chill for about 30 minutes, until cool and firm.

Sift together the buckwheat flour, rice flour, ground almonds, rapadura, salt and xanthan gum (if using), or pulse briefly in a food processor.

Pour the dry ingredients into a medium mixing bowl, add the chilled wet ingredients and blend together using a spatula or your fingertips. Knead gently to form a smooth, soft dough. Flatten, wrap in clingfilm (plastic wrap) and rest in the fridge for at least an hour or up to 3 days.

Divide the dough into 5 equal pieces before rolling out between 2 sheets of baking parchment until 3mm (⅛in) thick. Use it to line 5 x 10-cm (4-in) individual tart cases. Remove one piece of parchment, flip the pastry over and rest it on top of each tin. Peel off the remaining parchment, then press the pastry into the base and sides of the tin. Chill for 30 minutes.

Preheat the oven to 200°C/fan 180°C/400°F and put a baking sheet into the oven. Line the tart cases with baking parchment, then fill with rice. Place on the preheated tray and bake for 20 minutes, or until the edges of the pastry are just beginning to brown. Remove the parchment and rice and cook the cases for a further 3–4 minutes, or until the bases look dry. Cool in the tins. Remove the tart cases from the tins before filling.

Meanwhile, make the Vegan Pastry Cream.

For the rhubarb, bring the orange juice and sugar to the boil in a pan, stirring to dissolve the sugar. Add the rhubarb and shake the pan to coat. Cover and cook over a low heat for 1 minute, or until you can easily pierce it with a knife. Cool, still covered, then chill in the poaching liquid until needed.

Spoon the pastry cream into the tart case(s) and gently spread with the back of a spoon. Strain the rhubarb from the poaching liquid and place on top. Finish with Candied Orange Strips.

A posset is traditionally a mix of cream, citrus and sugar that is simply heated, mixed together and on cooling magically transforms to a thick dessert. With golden sugar and coconut cream instead of dairy cream, this version is lighter and a great simple option for vegans and anyone who is dairy-intolerant.

Lemon & Basil Posset

WF | GF | DF | VG

SERVES 4

finely grated zest and juice of
    1 lemon (about 80g/3oz juice)
5 basil leaves, roughly torn
90g (3¼oz/½ cup) golden caster
    (superfine) sugar or demerara
    (raw brown) sugar
30g (1oz/2 tbsp) coconut oil
350g (12¼oz/generous 1 cup)
    coconut cream, chilled
basil sprigs, to decorate

Heat the juice and zest in a small pan and simmer for 2–3 minutes until reduced by around half. Remove from the heat and add the torn basil leaves, along with the sugar and coconut oil. Mix well until the oil has melted and blended in, then cover and allow to infuse and cool for 1 hour.

Strain the lemon mixture over the cold coconut cream and stir thoroughly with a balloon whisk. Spoon into 4 ramekins or little pots. Cover and chill in the fridge for at least 4 hours before serving (it keeps well in the fridge for up to 3 days).

Decorate with a basil sprig and serve with fresh strawberries and cookies, such as the Buckwheat, Citrus & Lavender Sablés (see page 31).

This cake is another food memory reinvented. When I first moved to London to work as a pastry chef, I worked at Baker & Spice in Chelsea where we used to make wonderful orange and poppy seed loaves. No skimping on ingredients, we used organic eggs and plenty of French butter in the recipe. This loaf cake is definitely better for the waistline, but still has bags of flavour and moisture from the butternut squash and citrus zest.

Orange, Butternut & Poppy Seed Loaf

WF | GF | DF

MAKES I LOAF
to serve 4–6

70g (2½oz/½ cup) rice flour
20g (¾oz/¼ cup) finely ground
    oats or oat flour
65g (2¼oz/⅔ cup) ground almonds
1 tsp baking powder
⅛ tsp bicarbonate of soda
    (baking soda)
⅛ tsp xantham gum (optional)
½ butternut squash
finely grated zest of 1 large orange
finely grated zest of ½ lemon
1 tbsp lemon juice
1 tbsp poppy seeds
2 eggs
85g (3oz/7 tbsp) golden caster
    (granulated) sugar or demerara
    (raw brown) sugar
Candied Orange Slices (see page
    133), to decorate
coconut oil, for greasing

FOR THE GLACÉ ICING
120g (4½oz/¾ cup plus 2 tbsp)
    golden icing (confectioners')
    sugar
1 tsp poppy seeds
juice of ½ orange
juice of ¼ lemon

Preheat the oven to 180°C/fan 160°C/350°F. Grease a 450g (1lb) loaf tin with coconut oil and line the base and sides with baking parchment.

Sift together the flours, ground almonds, raising agents and xanthan gum, if using, and set aside.

Peel and coarsely grate the butternut squash. Weigh out 150g (5¼oz) and scatter over the zests, juices and poppy seeds.

In a separate bowl, whisk together the eggs and sugar until thick and doubled in volume. Gently fold through the butternut mixture lightly, followed by the dry ingredients, then leave for 10 minutes.

Scrape the batter into the tin and bake in the centre of the oven for 40 minutes, or until the top springs back when pressed and an inserted skewer or cocktail stick comes out clean.

Cool the cake in the tin for 10 minutes, then turn out and cool completely on a wire rack.

For the icing, sift the icing (confectioners') sugar into a bowl, add the poppy seeds and add enough juice to form an icing the thickness of double (heavy) cream. You probably will not need all of it. Pour the icing over the cooled cake and leave for a few minutes before decorating with the Candied Orange Slices.

My mother's favourite flower was lavender, and when I was younger I went through a stage of baking lavender cookies. They became a staple on my private chef jobs in the South of France, where lavender is in plentiful supply. This is a more wholesome version, packed with more nutrients than the original, but the flavour is still unmistakably that of Provence.

Buckwheat, Citrus & Lavender Sablés

WF | GF | DF | VG

MAKES 14 COOKIES
or 28 small cut-outs

2–3 tsp dried lavender flowers
60g (2¼oz/6 tbsp) demerara (raw brown) sugar
pinch of sea salt
70g (2½oz/½ cup) buckwheat flour
30g (1oz/¼ cup) teff flour
40g (1½oz/⅓ cup) rice flour
2 tsp ground flaxseed
60g (2¼oz/scant ⅔ cup) ground almonds
45g (1½oz/¼ cup) coconut oil
finely grated zest of ½ lemon
finely grated zest of ½ orange
2 tsp lemon juice

TO SERVE
icing (confectioners') sugar, for sprinkling
lavender sprigs

Mix the lavender with the sugar and set aside for a few hours or overnight. If you are short of time, skip this step.

Blitz the lavender, sugar and salt in a blender until fine. Sift together the flours, flaxseed and ground almonds with the lavender sugar into a bowl or a food processor. Add the coconut oil, zests and lemon juice and either rub through with your fingertips or pulse until the mixture clumps together like damp breadcrumbs. Turn out onto a work surface and use your hands to bring it together to form a smooth dough.

Turn the dough out onto a piece of baking parchment. Place another piece of parchment on top and roll out to an even thickness of 4mm (⅛in). If easier, you can divide the dough in half and do this in two parts. Place the rolled-out dough onto a flat tray lined with baking parchment and chill for at least 30 minutes or up to 3 days before cutting and baking.

When ready to bake, preheat the oven to 170°C/fan 150°C/340°F. Cut out shapes from the dough with a cookie cutter, or cut squares using a long straight knife. Re-form and re-roll excess dough and cut out more shapes. You should have enough dough for 14 medium cookies (roughly 9 x 5.5cm/3½ x 2¼in across) or 28 small cookies.

Place the cookies on a baking sheet and bake for 12 minutes for medium cookies or 10 minutes for small cookies. They should look dry and be a slightly darker brown around the edges. Cool on the tray. Store in an airtight container for up to 5 days at room temperature. Serve sprinkled with sugar and lavender sprigs.

I wanted to create a classic-style cheesecake that could be enjoyed by vegans and those who are gluten-intolerant. The finish is inspired by a cheesecake we used to make at Fifteen restaurant in London; baked vanilla with a layer of crème fraîche on top, so fresh and light. It was superlative, and while the extra stage is a tiny bit more time and effort, it really completes the pudding.

Vanilla Cheesecake

WF | GF | DF | VG

MAKES A 15-CM (6-IN) CHEESECAKE
to serve 6–8

1 quantity of Cheesecake Base
(see page 131)

FOR THE FILLING
120g (4¼oz/1 cup) cashew nuts
pinch of sea salt
80g (3oz/scant ½ cup) coconut
oil, melted
100g (3½oz/⅓ cup) maple syrup
2 tsp cider vinegar
200g (7oz/¾ cup) coconut cream
1 vanilla pod (bean), halved
lengthways and seeds scraped
out or 1 tbsp vanilla paste

FOR THE TOPPING
200g (7oz/⅓ cup) coconut cream,
at room temperature
1 tsp maple syrup
½ tsp cider vinegar
1 tsp melted coconut oil
edible flowers, to decorate

Line the base of a 15-cm (6-in) springform tin with baking parchment. Make the Cheesecake Base according to the method on page 131, baking in the lined tin.

For the filling, soak the cashews in cold water for 1 hour. Drain and blend in a blender or food processor with the salt until as fine as possible. Add the coconut oil and blend again until completely smooth. Add the remaining ingredients and blend again until well mixed and smooth. Fill the tin and chill until just firm. This takes 2 hours in the freezer or overnight in the fridge.

For the topping, blend all the ingredients together with a balloon whisk. Gently pour onto the cheesecake and tap to remove any air bubbles. Return to the fridge or freezer to set for a few hours. For best results, chill overnight until firm and creamy.

To de-mould, warm the sides of the tin with a hot damp tea towel or blowtorch, then unclip the sides and slide the cheesecake off the base. The cheesecake will keep well in the fridge for 3–4 days, and becomes firmer with time. Decorate with edible flowers to serve.

TIP:
For a neater finish when de-moulding, place the cheesecake in the freezer for half an hour.

I love baking cakes in mini moulds, and silicone cannelé moulds are perfect for these little treats. The cakes stay bite-sized, and the gluten-free batter bakes better in the smaller sizes. The natural sweetness of parsnip pairs perfectly with the tart passion fruit, and the finish is bright, colourful and mood-lifting!

Passion Fruit & Parsnip Mini Cakes

WF | GF | DF

MAKES 12 CAKES

about 1 large parsnip
3 large ripe passion fruit
(or 4 if they are small)
2 eggs
60g (2¼oz/⅓ cup) golden caster (granulated) sugar or demerara (raw brown) sugar
80g (3oz/⅓ cup) rapeseed (canola) oil or melted coconut oil
60g (2¼oz/¼ cup) honey
50g (1¾oz/⅓ cup) brown rice flour
50g (1¾oz/½ cup) ground almonds
½ tsp ground psyllium husk (optional)
1½ tsp baking powder

FOR THE PASSION FRUIT GLAZE

150g (5¼oz/1 cup) golden icing (confectioners') sugar
remaining passion fruit juice and seeds
dried calendula petals, to finish

Wash (but don't peel) the parsnip and grate it finely, grating around the outside and avoiding the inner woody part. You need 150g (5¼oz) grated parsnip.

If the passion fruit are not perfectly ripe (very wrinkly), then warm them for 30 seconds in the microwave. Cut them open and strain the passion fruit pulp through a sieve, pressing down to extract as much juice as possible. Pour 35g (1fl oz/2 tbsp) of the juice over the grated parsnip and set aside. Scoop 1 tbsp of the seeds into the remaining juice and set aside.

Whisk together the eggs and caster (granulated) sugar on medium-high speed for 5 minutes, or until pale and doubled in volume. Keep whisking the eggs on high speed, then pour in the oil a little at a time, down the side of the bowl. Once incorporated, whisk in the honey.

Fold in the grated parsnip using a silicone spatula until well incorporated. Sift together the flour, ground almonds, psyllium husk, if using, and baking powder, then fold through the cake batter. Leave for 10 minutes.

Preheat the oven to 170°C/fan 150°C/325°F. Lightly grease a 12-hole cannelé or silicone mould with rapeseed (canola) or coconut oil and place on a baking sheet.

Scrape the batter into a jug and fill the moulds to just below the top. Leave for 5 minutes, then bake for 25 minutes, or until browned and the tops spring back when gently pressed, but the sponge still feels soft to the touch. Cool the cakes in the moulds on a wire rack for 10 minutes, then de-mould and cool.

For the glaze, sift the icing (confectioners') sugar into a bowl and add the passion fruit juice and seeds. Add enough hot water to form a glacé icing, the thickness of double (heavy) cream. Spoon 1 teaspoon on top of each cake and pull the edges out to achieve drips down the sides. Sprinkle calendula petals on top before the icing sets.

This roulade is perfect for late spring or early summer, when rhubarb is still in season and the first of the local strawberries are appearing. Best eaten on the day it's made but still messily delicious the next day!

Rhubarb, Strawberry & Parsnip Roulade

WF | GF | DF

SERVES 6-8

4 medium egg whites (about 135g/4¾oz)
pinch of sea salt
105g (3¾oz/½ cup) golden caster (superfine) sugar
65g (2¼oz) finely grated parsnip
finely grated zest of 1 unwaxed lemon
60g (2¼oz/½ cup) rice flour
45g (1½oz/½ cup) ground almonds
coconut oil, for greasing

FOR THE COMPOTE

160g (5¾oz) rhubarb, chopped into 2-cm (¾-in) lengths
juice of ½ lemon
100g (3½oz/½ cup) golden caster (granulated) sugar or demerara (raw brown) sugar
130g (4½oz/1 cup) strawberries, hulled and quartered
4 tsp agar agar

FOR THE COCONUT CHANTILLY CREAM

150g (5¼oz/½ cup) coconut cream, chilled
1 tbsp golden icing (confectioners') sugar
1 tsp vanilla paste or ½ vanilla pod (bean), halved lengthways and seeds scraped out

TO DECORATE

3–4 strawberries, halved

Preheat the oven to 180°C/fan 160°C/350°F. Grease a 38 x 26-cm (15 x 10½-in) Swiss (jelly) roll tin with coconut oil and line with baking parchment.

Whisk the egg whites with the salt until light and foamy; they should hold a firm peak. Sprinkle on one-quarter of the sugar and whisk for 20 seconds until incorporated, then add the next quarter of sugar and whisk again. Add the remaining sugar in the same way, then whisk for 1 minute until glossy and thick.

Add the parsnip and lemon zest and fold through until just incorporated. Sift together the flour and ground almonds and gently fold into the mixture. Pour into the tin and spread out evenly. Bake for 12–15 minutes, or until puffed up and springs back when pressed. Cool in the tin on a wire rack until cold.

For the compote, gently heat the rhubarb, lemon juice and sugar in a covered pan for 4–5 minutes until the rhubarb is almost tender. Add the strawberries and leave on the heat for another minute. Remove and cool. When the fruit has cooled, strain through a sieve, pressing down gently. Place the juices in a small pan and add the agar agar. Gently bring to the boil and simmer, stirring for 4–5 minutes until thickened. Add the fruit to the pan and mix well. Cool, then chill well.

For the Chantilly cream, gently whisk together the coconut cream, icing (confectioners') sugar and vanilla, until billowy but still stiff. If it becomes too loose, chill to firm up.

To assemble, place the sponge upside down, shortest side closest to you, on top of a piece of baking parchment, and peel off the backing paper. Spread with a layer of the compote, leaving a 2.5cm (1in) border at the top, then spread over most of the cream. Use the baking parchment to lift and roll it tightly from the bottom. Once rolled, set the roulade on a plate and pipe the remaining cream on top. Decorate with halved strawberries.

Vibrant
+ FRUITY

The quality of the mangoes makes a difference with this dessert, so pick the best-quality and ripest you can find. This is a super-tangy and bright cheesecake that needs nothing extra with it, except maybe a little passion fruit pulp and edible flowers to top it off if you're feeling colourful.

Mango & Passion Fruit Cheesecake

WF | GF | DF | VG

MAKES 8 INDIVIDUAL CHEESECAKES

1 quantity of Cheesecake Base
  (see page 131)
95g (3¼oz/¾ cup) cashew nuts
5 ripe passion fruit, about
  40–45g (1½oz)
2 medium ripe mangoes, peeled,
  chopped and puréed, about
  340g (12oz)
pinch of salt
80g (3oz/scant ½ cup) coconut oil,
  melted
75g (2¾oz/¼ cup) brown rice syrup
  (for vegans) or honey
80g (3oz/¼ cup) coconut cream

Make the Cheesecake Base according to the instructions on page 131, using an 8-hole round silicone mould (each about 5cm/2in diameter).

For the filling, soak the cashews in cold water for 1 hour.

Meanwhile, cut the passion fruit open and strain the pulp through a fine sieve into a bowl, pressing down well to extract as much juice as possible. Reserve 1 tablespoon of the pulp. Add the juice to a small pan along with the mango purée and cook over a medium-low heat for 10–15 minutes until the purée has reduced and thickened. Weigh out 240g (8½oz) of the purée and set aside to cool.

Drain the cashews and blend in a blender with the salt until as fine as possible. Add the coconut oil and blend again until smooth. Add the syrup or honey, cooled fruit purée and the coconut cream and blend until smooth. Mix in the reserved passion fruit pulp by hand.

Fill the cavities of the silicone moulds to the top and chill the cheesecakes overnight before de-moulding and serving, or in the freezer for 2 or more hours. If frozen, they are easier to de-mould, but leave to soften in the fridge for an hour or two before serving. They will keep well in a covered container in the fridge for 2–3 days.

Everything about this cake shouts summer – from the super bright, orangey-yellow sponge to the light and fluffy cream and seasonal berries. This cake has mood-lifting goodness running through it, and the vegetables help to keep it light and moist, so a big slice is a rewarding treat, rather than weighing you down on a hot day.

Summer Berry Layer Cake with Coconut Cream

WF | GF | DF

MAKES A 15-CM (6-IN) CAKE
to serve 6–8

FOR THE SPONGE
1 small yellow courgette (zucchini)
⅛ butternut squash
finely grated zest 1 of lemon
1 tbsp lemon juice
pinch of sea salt
120g (4¼oz/⅔ cup minus 2 tsp)
  golden caster (granulated) or
  demerara (raw brown) sugar
2 eggs
100g (3½oz/¾ cup) rice flour
40g (1½oz/scant ½ cup) ground
  almonds
2 tsp ground flaxseed
½ tsp bicarbonate of soda
  (baking soda)
1 egg white
rapeseed (canola) or coconut oil,
  for greasing

For the sponge, grate (but don't peel) the courgettes (zucchini) coarsely. Layer the grated courgette up between double thicknesses of kitchen paper or tea towels and press down to extract the juice. Allow to dry for about 30 minutes, making sure the courgette is well drained. Prepare the squash in the same way, avoiding the skin and seeds. Weigh out 120g (4¼oz) courgette and 90g (3¼oz) squash, then add the lime zest and juice to this.

Add the salt and 100g (3½oz/ ½ cup) of the sugar to the whole eggs in a separate bowl, then whisk on medium-high speed for 5 minutes, or until pale and doubled in volume. Fold through the grated vegetables until well incorporated. Sift together the flour, ground almonds, flaxseed

and bicarbonate of soda (baking soda), and fold through the cake batter. Leave for 10 minutes.

Preheat the oven to 180°C/fan 160°C/350°F.

Grease 2 x 15-cm (6-in) round sandwich tins with rapeseed (canola) or coconut oil and line with baking parchment. Whisk the egg white with the remaining sugar to make a soft peak meringue, then fold into the cake batter. Divide the batter evenly between the tins and bake for 30 minutes, or until browned and the tops spring back when gently pressed.

Allow the cakes to cool in their tins on a wire rack until just warm. Remove from the tins and cool on the rack until cold. Chill before slicing and filling.

ingredients and method continue overleaf

FOR THE COCONUT CHANTILLY CREAM

250g (8¾oz/scant 1 cup) coconut
  cream, chilled
2 tbsp golden icing (confectioners')
  sugar
2 tsp vanilla paste or a vanilla pod
  (bean), halved lengthways and
  seeds scraped out

TO ASSEMBLE THE CAKE

250g (8¾oz/2 cups) mixed summer
  berries, such as raspberries,
  strawberries and blueberries
mint sprigs
golden icing (confectioners') sugar,
  for dusting (optional)

For the Chantilly cream, gently whip together the coconut cream, icing (confectioners') sugar and vanilla with a whisk, until billowy but still stiff. If it becomes too loose, chill until firm.

Slice the top of the sponges so they are straight and remove the baking parchment from the bottom. Place the first sponge on a serving plate or cake board, and spoon a little coconut cream on top, followed by a small handful of berries. Top with the next sponge, bottom crust side up, and spread the remaining cream on top. Sprinkle with the remaining berries, the mint and dust with icing sugar, if liked.

Gooseberry and elderflower have such a short season, but they coincide perfectly in early summer. This cake makes the most of the seasonal synergy; but if you're not at just the right time of year, you can use frozen gooseberries for the compote and bottled elderflower cordial is available year-round.

Courgette, Gooseberry & Elderflower Layer Cake

WF | GF | DF

MAKES A 15-CM (6-IN) CAKE
to serve 6–8

FOR THE CAKE
2 medium courgettes (zucchini)
finely grated zest of 1 lime
150g (5¼oz/¾ cup) golden caster
    (granulated) sugar or demerara
    (raw brown) sugar
pinch of sea salt
3 eggs
100g (3½oz/¾ cup) rice flour
40g (1½oz/⅓ cup) teff flour
60g (2¼oz/⅔ cup) ground almonds
3 tsp ground flaxseed
¾ tsp bicarbonate of soda
    (baking soda)
rapeseed (canola) or coconut oil for
    greasing

FOR THE GOOSEBERRY COMPOTE
250g (8¾oz/2¼ cups) gooseberries,
    topped and tailed
3 tbsp elderflower cordial
1 tsp agar flakes
50g (1¾oz/¼ cup) golden
    granulated sugar or demerara
    (raw brown) sugar

For the cake, grate (but don't peel) the courgettes (zucchini) coarsely. Layer the grated courgette up between double thicknesses of kitchen paper or clean tea towels and press down to extract the juice. Allow to dry for about 30 minutes, making sure the courgette is well drained. Weigh out 275g (9¾oz) into a bowl, and add the lime zest to this.

Add the sugar and salt to the eggs in a separate bowl, then whisk on medium-high speed for 5 minutes, or until pale and doubled in volume. Fold through the grated courgette using a silicone spatula, until well incorporated. Sift together both flours, the ground almonds, flaxseed and bicarbonate of soda (baking soda) and fold through the cake batter. Leave for 10 minutes.

Preheat the oven to 180°C/fan 160°C/350°F.

Grease 3 x 15-cm (6-in) round sandwich tins with rapeseed (canola) or coconut oil and line the bases with baking parchment. Divide the batter evenly between the tins and bake for 35 minutes, or until browned and the tops spring back when gently pressed.

Allow the cakes to cool still in the tins on a wire rack until just warm. Remove from the tins and cool on the rack until cold. Chill before filling.

For the compote, place the gooseberries in a small pan with the cordial and sprinkle the agar flakes on top. Leave for 5 minutes for the flakes to absorb the liquid, then heat without stirring until the mixture just

ingredients and method continue overleaf

FOR THE ELDERFLOWER CREAM

350g (12¼oz/1½ cups) coconut
    cream, chilled
1–2 tbsp elderflower cordial

TO ASSEMBLE THE CAKE

2–3 tbsp elderflower cordial
fresh elderflowers, to decorate

comes to the boil. Add the sugar and cook gently until dissolved. Simmer stirring occasionally for 10 minutes until the fruit is softened and the agar has dissolved. It will still look runny, but thickens on cooling. Scrape into a bowl and cool until thickened. Cover and chill until needed.

For the cream, mix the coconut cream and cordial together and whisk lightly until aerated and thick. If it is too loose, chill before layering.

To assemble, slice the top of the sponges so they are straight and remove the baking parchment

from the bottom. Place the first sponge on a serving plate or cake board, and brush a little of the cordial on top. Pipe or spoon the elderflower cream in intervals on top and fill in the gaps with the gooseberry compote. Top with the next sponge, brush with cordial and top in the same way with the cream and compote.

Place the final layer of sponge with the bottom crust side up, and brush with any remaining cordial. Pipe the remaining cream on top in large peaks and dot with the remaining compote. Decorate with elderflowers and serve.

TIP:
Because of the cream filling, any leftovers should be stored in the fridge. The cake will keep well in a covered container for a couple of days.

Pancakes are not just for the weekend! This recipe is a regular at home; one I created for my sister to enjoy when she needed a gluten-free, dairy-free treat. They really are a wholesome breakfast choice: plenty of fibre and protein from the buckwheat and ground almonds, prebiotics from the banana and digestive balance from the psyllium. Top with fresh berries and your choice of yoghurt for extra vitamins and protein.

Banana Buckwheat Pancakes

WF | GF | DF | VG

MAKES 8 PANCAKES

150g (5¼oz/scant 1 cup)
    buckwheat flour
50g (1¾oz/½ cup) ground almonds
2 tsp baking powder
½ tsp ground psyllium (optional)
½ tsp ground cinnamon
about 2 small bananas
260g (8¾fl oz/1 cup) unsweetened
    almond milk (or your choice of
    dairy-free milk)
1 tbsp maple syrup
pinch of sea salt
1 tsp cider vinegar
20g (¾fl oz/4 tsp) rapeseed (canola)
    oil or melted coconut oil, plus
    extra for frying

TO SERVE
about 300g (10½oz/2½ cups) mixed
    fresh berries
your choice of maple syrup,
    coconut nectar or rice syrup

For the pancakes, sift together the flour, ground almonds, baking powder, psyllium, if using, and cinnamon into a bowl.

Weigh the bananas – you need 110g (4oz) – and mash well. Mix the banana with the remaining ingredients, then pour this into the dry ingredients and blend well with a balloon whisk. Rest for 20 minutes, or cover and chill for up to 2 days.

Melt a little coconut oil, or rapeseed (canola) oil in a pan and add a few tablespoons of the pancake batter. Fry over a medium heat for 2 minutes, or until the underneath is browned and you can see bubbles on the surface. Flip over and cook for another minute or so until browned underneath. Remove and keep warm in a low oven, covered with a tea towel while you fry the rest.

Serve with berries and your choice of syrup. I love these with coconut yoghurt as well!

This take on a carrot cake plays with Middle Eastern flavours, rather than the classic spices. It is a lighter, more summery version, and works perfectly baked in small silicone moulds.

Carrot, Orange & Pistachio Cakes

WF | GF | DF

MAKES 8 SMALL CAKES

FOR THE CAKES
70g (2½oz/½ cup) brown rice flour
30g (1oz/¼ cup) buckwheat flour
30g (1oz/⅓ cup) ground almonds
½ tsp bicarbonate of soda
   (baking soda)
¼ tsp ground nutmeg
½ tsp ground turmeric
pinch of sea salt
1 tsp ground flaxseed
185g (6½oz) carrots
finely grated zest of 1 orange
finely grated zest of ½ lemon
20g (¾fl oz/4 tsp) orange juice
2 tsp lemon juice
30g (1oz/¼ cup) pistachios,
   roughly chopped
2 eggs
120g (4¼oz/⅔ cup minus 2 tsp)
   golden caster (granulated) or
   demerara (raw brown) sugar

FOR THE ROSEWATER COCONUT CREAM
250g (8¾oz/scant 1 cup) coconut
   cream, chilled
2 tbsp golden icing (confectioners')
   sugar
few drops of rosewater or
   rose extract

TO DECORATE
chopped pistachios
rose petals

Preheat the oven to 180°C/fan 160°C/350°F. Grease an 8-hole oval silicone financier/friand mould (cavity dimensions about 7.5 x 5.5cm/3 x 2¼in) with a little coconut oil.

For the cakes, sift together the flours, ground almonds, bicarbonate of soda (baking soda), spices, salt and flaxseed in a mixing bowl and set aside. Grate the carrots into a separate bowl and top with the zests, juices and pistachios.

Whisk together the eggs and sugar until thick and doubled in volume. Fold through the carrot mixture lightly, followed by the dry ingredients using a rubber spatula. Be careful to fold just enough to lightly mix, so you don't lose too much air. Leave for 10 minutes to allow the starches to absorb the liquid.

Use a piping bag or jug to fill the moulds evenly, then bake in the centre of the oven for 30 minutes, or until the tops spring back when pressed and an inserted skewer or cocktail stick comes out clean. Cool slightly in the mould, then turn out and cool completely on a wire rack.

For the cream, gently whip together the coconut cream, icing (confectioners') sugar and rosewater with a whisk, until just aerated but still stiff. If it becomes too loose, chill until firm. Taste to check the rosewater flavour – a little goes a long way, but add more if you feel it needs it.

Place the cream into a piping bag fitted with your choice of nozzle and pipe a swirl or peak on top of each cake. Decorate with a few extra chopped pistachios and rose petals.

This is a classic flavour combination, made into a summery tart with the added bonus of being vegan, a good source of vitamin C and of antioxidants. The balsamic reduction adds a luxurious extra dark note, but can be left out if you want to keep things simple. Serve this alfresco to give friends a true taste of summer.

Strawberry & Basil Tart

WF | GF | DF | VG

MAKES 5 SMALL TARTS

1 quantity of Pastry (see page 130)
1 quantity of Vegan Pastry Cream (see page 131)
250–300g (8¾–10½oz/2½–3 cups) fresh strawberries, hulled and halved or quartered
juice of ¼ lemon
1 tsp brown rice syrup or maple syrup
small basil sprigs

FOR THE BALSAMIC REDUCTION

40g (1½fl oz/3 tbsp) best-quality balsamic vinegar
45g (1½oz/3¼ tbsp) rapadura or light muscovado (soft brown) sugar
2–3 strawberries, finely chopped

Make the Pastry according to the instructions on page 130, using it to line 5 x 10cm (4in) individual tart tins.

Preheat the oven to 200°C/fan 180°C/400°F and put a baking sheet into the oven to heat. Line the bases of the tarts with baking parchment, then fill with rice or lentils. Gather the edges of the parchment together loosely in the centre and bake on the tray for 20 minutes, or until the edges of the pastry are beginning to brown. Remove the rice and cook the cases for a further 3–4 minutes, or until the bases look dry. Cool in the tins on a wire rack until cold. Remove the tart cases from the tins before filling.

Make the Vegan Pastry Cream according to the instructions on page 131.

Heat all the ingredients for the balsamic reduction gently until the sugar has dissolved and the strawberries are mushy. Bring to the boil, then reduce the heat and simmer for 4–5 minutes, until it has reduced slightly and become syrupy. Strain and cool.

To assemble, mix together the strawberries, lemon juice and syrup. Fill each tart case two-thirds full with the pastry cream, then tumble the strawberries on top. Sprinkle basil leaves on top, then serve with the balsamic reduction.

This tart works equally well as a refreshing summer dessert or alternative winter pudding. I first served this for a Christmas party with gluten- and egg-intolerant guests, and brought it out again for a summer party six months later! The stem (preserved) ginger cookies are great here, since they are gluten- and dairy-free, but you can use any ginger cookies you like – just check that they work with any allergies you may be catering for.

Ginger-chocolate & Orange Frozen Tart

WF | GF | DF | VG

MAKES A 20-CM (8-IN) TART

FOR THE CRUST
45g (1½oz/¼ cup) coconut oil
65g (2¼oz) vegan dark chocolate
   (70% cocoa solids)
15g (½oz/1 tbsp) maple syrup
200g (7oz) gluten-free stem
   (preserved) ginger cookies

FOR THE FILLING
juice of 1 orange, about 90g
   (3fl oz/⅓ cup)
juice of 1 lime, about 40g
   (1½oz/3 tbsp)
finely grated zest of 1 orange
   and 1 lime
40g (1½oz/¼ cup) coconut
   oil, melted
130g (4½oz/⅔ cup) golden icing
   (confectioners') sugar
350g (12¼oz/1 cup) coconut cream
Candied Orange Slices (see page
   133), to decorate

Gently melt together the coconut oil and chocolate in the microwave or in a heatproof bowl over a pan of simmering water. Once melted, add the maple syrup and stir thoroughly.

Process the ginger cookies in a blender or food processor until fine. Tip into a bowl, add the chocolate mixture and blend well with a silicone spatula.

Line the base of a 20-cm (8-in) loose-based tart tin with a circle of baking parchment. Tip the chocolate crust mixture into the centre and use your fingertips to press into the bottom and up the sides until it is evenly lined. Place in the freezer while you make the filling.

For the filling, mix together the juices, zests, coconut oil and icing (confectioners') sugar.

In a separate bowl, whip the coconut cream with a hand-held electric whisk for 30 seconds to loosen, add the juice mix, and whip again for 1–2 minutes until well-blended and forming soft peaks. Tip the mixture into the well-chilled tart case, spread out evenly and freeze for 4–5 hours until firm.

Before serving, place the tart in the fridge for 30 minutes to soften slightly. Decorate with Candied Orange Slices, then remove from the tart case and cut with a large warmed knife.

This recipe was inspired by a sea salt and olive oil mousse I once had at the Lido in Bristol. Halfway between a mousse and a chocolate pot, this dessert is decadent and creamy. The avocado provides a great nutritional boost, as well as a rich creamy texture, and the flavour pairs perfectly with the olive oil.

Olive Oil & Avocado Chocolate Mousse

WF | GF | DF | VG

SERVES 2

100g (3½oz) vegan dark chocolate (70% cocoa solids), broken into pieces

50g (1¾oz/⅓ cup) pitted dates (Medjool if possible)

55g (1¾fl oz/¼ cup) maple syrup or rice syrup

1 medium avocado (100g/ 3½oz flesh)

40g (1½fl oz/3 tbsp) extra virgin olive oil, plus extra for drizzling

large pinch of sea salt, plus extra for sprinkling

100g (3½oz/⅓ cup) coconut cream

Melt the chocolate in a heatproof bowl set over a pan of barely simmering water. Once melted, allow to cool slightly.

Process the dates in a blender until smooth, add the syrup and process again. Halve and scoop the flesh from the avocado and add this, along with the olive oil and salt to the blender and process again until smooth. Scrape in the melted cooled chocolate and blend again until smooth. Lastly, add the coconut cream, blend together, then scrape the mixture into 2 small ramekins or coffee cups.

Chill in the fridge for about 2–3 hours until set. Serve with a sprinkle of sea salt and a drizzle of extra olive oil on top.

A friand, or financier, is an egg white and almond-based sponge that is simple to make, and the unbaked batter can be kept in the fridge for a while before use. This makes it the ultimate low-effort, high-reward bake, and this version is gluten- and dairy-free to boot. The combination of peach, rosemary and olive oil is pure summer, but you can easily substitute other stone fruit or herbs – try thyme and plum or lavender and apricot.

Peach, Rosemary & Olive Oil Friands

WF | GF | DF

MAKES 8 FRIANDS

2 rosemary sprigs, finely chopped, 1 tsp reserved for topping
110g (4oz/½ cup, plus 1 tbsp) demerara (raw brown) sugar
85g (3oz/generous ¾ cup) ground almonds
40g (1½oz/¼ cup) brown rice flour or rice flour
5g (⅛oz/1 tbsp) cornflour (cornstarch) or tapioca flour
½ tsp baking powder
4 egg whites (about 140g/5oz)
40g (1½oz/3 tbsp) extra virgin olive oil
80g (3oz/⅓ cup) dairy-free yoghurt
finely grated zest of 1 lemon
1 tsp lemon juice
1 firm ripe peach, sliced into 16 pieces
warm honey, for glazing
rapeseed (canola) or coconut oil, for greasing

Blitz the finely chopped rosemary with the sugar in a blender until fine.

Sift together the rosemary-sugar, ground almonds, flours and baking powder into a bowl. Add the egg whites and stir gently with a whisk.

Mix together the olive oil, yoghurt, lemon zest and juice. Add to the batter and blend gently with the whisk. Scrape the mixture into a piping bag or jug, cover and chill for at least 30 minutes, or up to 24 hours.

When ready to bake, preheat the oven to 180°C/fan 160°C/350°F.

Grease an 8-hole oval silicone financier/friand mould (each cavity dimensions about 7.5 x 5.5cm/3 x 2¼in) with rapeseed (canola) or melted coconut oil and place on a baking sheet. Pour or pipe the batter into each cavity to fill two-thirds, then top each with 2 slices of peach. Bake for 35 minutes, or until risen and browned around the edges.

Cool the cakes still in the moulds on a wire rack for 10 minutes, then de-mould and cool completely. Glaze with a little warm honey, then sprinkle the reserved rosemary on top. They will keep for 2 days in an airtight container in the fridge.

This works particularly well with any leftover Lemon & Earl Grey Loaf Cakes (see page 22), but you can use any cake you like, as long as it pairs well with the vanilla, raspberries and nectarine. My parents used to grow raspberries in the garden at home, so we always had them as a regular standby for our summer trifles. I have made this version even more summery with the addition of nectarine.

Simple Summer Trifle

WF | GF | DF

SERVES 6

1 quantity of Custard (see page 132)
2 individual Lemon & Earl Grey Loaf Cakes (see page 22), cut into small slices
15g (½fl oz/1 tbsp) lemon juice
15g (½oz/4 tsp) demerara (raw brown) sugar
75g (2¾oz/½ cup plus 2 tbsp) fresh raspberries
1 ripe nectarine, stoned and cut into pieces
300g (10½oz/1¼ cup) coconut cream, chilled
15g (½oz/⅛ cup) pistachios, chopped
toasted flaked (silvered) almonds or grated chocolate, to decorate

Make the Custard according to the instructions on page 132.

Arrange the cake slices in the base of your chosen dish. Heat together the lemon juice and sugar until dissolved, then sprinkle on top of the cake. Add the raspberries and nectarine pieces. Top with the slightly warm custard, removing the vanilla pod, and tap the bowl to even out and remove any bubbles. Chill the trifle until cold and the custard is set, about 1 hour.

Whip the chilled coconut cream until smooth, then spoon on top of the trifle. Top with chopped pistachios, toasted flaked (slivered) almonds or grated chocolate. The trifle will keep well in the fridge, covered, for up to 3 days.

TIP:
If you want to make this a little more grown-up. add a little Chambord or Limoncello into the lemon syrup before drizzling on top of the sponges. Then layer the trifle components in individual glasses for a more sophisticated look.

I love the colour in this tart! Use fresh and firm raspberries for the best effect when you slice into it. If pastry isn't your favourite thing, the filling also makes a great potted dessert by itself – simply pour into small ramekins and chill for a few hours before serving.

Pistachio & Raspberry Tart

WF | GF | DF | VG

MAKES A 20-CM (8-IN) TART

1 quantity of Pastry (see page 130)
65g (2¼oz/½ cup) pistachios
pinch of sea salt
50g (1¾oz/¼ cup) coconut oil, melted
70g (2½oz/¼ cup) brown rice syrup (for vegans) or honey
2½ tsp lemon juice
130g (4½oz/scant ½ cup) coconut cream
100g (3½oz/scant 1 cup) fresh raspberries
handful of pistachios, finely chopped, to decorate

Make the Pastry according to the instructions on page 130, using it to line a 20cm (8in) tart tin.

Preheat the oven to 200°C/fan 180°C/400°F and put a baking sheet into the oven to heat. Line the base of the tart case with baking parchment, then fill with rice or lentils. Gather the edges of the parchment together loosely in the centre and bake on the tray for 30 minutes, or until the edges of the pastry are beginning to brown. Remove the rice and cook for a further 6–7 minutes, or until the base looks dry. Cool in the tin on a wire rack until cold.

Meanwhile, for the filling, soak the pistachios in cold water for 1 hour.

Drain the pistachios and blend with the salt in a blender until as fine as possible. Add the coconut oil and blend again until completely smooth. Add the syrup or honey, lemon juice and coconut cream and blend again, until well mixed and smooth.

Place the raspberries on the base of the baked tart case and pour the filling on top. If the raspberries are large, press them down slightly so the filling can cover them. Chill for a few hours before de-moulding from the tin and serving decorated with finely chopped pistachios. The tart will keep in a covered container in the fridge for 2–3 days.

In one of the estates I worked on as a private chef near Toulouse, the garden was full of fig trees. In late August, this was the perfect time to pick and eat them, and we had them in everything! This is a 'healthy' homage to those figs. If you are ever going to bring out dessert wine, then this is the time to do it!

Fig & Honey Tart

WF | GF | DF | VG

MAKES 5 SMALL TARTS

FOR THE PASTRY
2 tsp gram (chickpea) flour
2 tsp ground flaxseed
70g (2½oz//⅓ cup) coconut cream
45g (1½oz/¼ cup) coconut oil
1 tsp cider vinegar
finely grated zest of 1 orange
100g (3½oz/generous ¾ cup)
   buckwheat flour
40g (1½oz/⅓ cup) rice flour
60g (2¼oz/⅔ cup) ground almonds
60g (2¼oz/5 tbsp) rapadura
   or light muscovado (soft
   brown) sugar
large pinch of sea salt
¼ tsp xanthan gum (optional)

TO ASSEMBLE
1 quantity of Vegan Pastry Cream
   (see page 131)
about 15 small figs
50g (1¾oz/⅛ cup) runny honey
seeds of 1 vanilla pod (bean) or
   1 tbsp vanilla paste

For the pastry, whisk together the gram flour, flaxseed, coconut cream, oil, cider vinegar and orange zest in a bowl until well blended. Chill for about 30 minutes, until cool and firm.

Sift together the buckwheat flour, rice flour, ground almonds, rapadura, salt and xanthan gum (if using), or pulse briefly in a food processor.

Pour the dry ingredients into a medium mixing bowl, add the chilled wet ingredients and blend together using a spatula or your fingertips. Knead gently to form a smooth, soft dough. Flatten, wrap in clingfilm (plastic wrap) and rest in the fridge for at least an hour or up to 3 days.

Divide the dough into 5 equal pieces and roll each one out between 2 sheets of baking parchment until 3mm (⅛in) thick. Use it to line 5 individual tart tins, about 10cm (4in) across. Chill for 30 minutes.

Preheat the oven to 200°C/fan 180°C/400°F and put a baking sheet into the oven to heat. Line the bases of the tart tins with baking parchment, then fill with rice or lentils. Gather the edges of the parchment together loosely in the centre and bake on the tray for 20 minutes, or until the edges of the pastry are just beginning to brown. Remove the rice and bake the cases for a further 3–4 minutes, or until the bases look dry. Cool in the tins on a wire rack until cold.

Make the Vegan Pastry Cream according to the instructions on page 131, then set aside.

To assemble, preheat the oven to 200°C/fan 180°C/400°F and line a baking sheet with foil. Cut the figs in half and place, cut side up, on the tray. Mix together the honey and vanilla seeds, then drizzle this on top of the figs. Roast for 10 minutes, or until just starting to colour at the edges. Cool until just warm.

Fill the tart cases with the cold pastry cream, then top with the warm figs.

Warm
+ NUTTY

I first created this recipe with the intention of adding rye flour, and found that the sweet potato was enough to hold the squidgy cake mixture together by itself. It also means you can do without lots of additional sugar usually needed for the fudgy texture; giving you the perfect brownie consistency with plenty of nutritional plus points.

Pecan-studded Sweet Potato Brownies

WF | GF | DF

MAKES 12 BROWNIES

1 large sweet potato, at least 350g (12oz) weight
150g (5¼oz/1⅓ cups) pecans
50g (1¾oz/⅓ cup) soft pitted dates (ideally Medjool)
200g (7oz) dark chocolate (70% cocoa solids), roughly chopped
50g (1¾fl oz/3½ tbsp) rapeseed (canola) oil
40g (1½oz/2½ tbsp) light tahini
3 eggs
160g (5¾oz/¾ cup plus 1 tbsp) coconut sugar or dark muscovado (soft brown) sugar
pinch of sea salt, plus a little extra for sprinkling
rapeseed (canola) oil, for greasing

Preheat the oven to 200°C/fan 180°C/400°F. Roast the sweet potato on a baking sheet for 45 minutes–1 hour, or until tender in the centre and slightly caramelizing on the outside. Meanwhile, toast the pecans on a baking sheet for 5–6 minutes until lightly browned. Cool, then roughly chop.

Reduce the oven temperature to 180°C/fan 160°C/350°F. Grease a 28 x 18-cm (11 x 7-in) brownie tin with a little rapeseed (canola) oil and line with baking parchment.

Let the potato cool until just warm, then peel and weigh out 200g (7oz) of the flesh into a blender. Add the dates and blend until smooth, then transfer the mixture to a heatproof bowl with the chocolate and set over a pan of barely simmering water. Heat, stirring occasionally, until the chocolate is melted. Add the oil and tahini and stir until smooth. Cool slightly.

Whisk the eggs, coconut sugar and salt on medium-high speed for 5 minutes, or until paler and almost doubled in volume, then whisk in the chocolate mixture slowly until well blended. Fold through most of the pecans.

Scrape the mix into the tin, gently levelling off the top. Scatter the remaining pecans over the top. Sprinkle with a large pinch of sea salt, then bake for 22–25 minutes, or until puffed and looking dry on top.

Cool in the tin before slicing into squares, or resist the temptation to be tidy and cut into random pieces! Chill any leftovers in a covered container for up to 3 days.

Caramel and chocolate are a classic combination, and these little cakes look and taste really indulgent! The butternut helps to add extra nutrients as well as keep the sponge moist, the dates add stickiness as well as extra fibre, and the chocolate is a natural stimulant and mood booster. This chocolatey treat doesn't leave you feeling guilty or sluggish afterwards.

Caramel & Chocolate Mini-Cakes

WF | GF | DF

MAKES 8 SMALL CAKES

FOR THE CAKES

¼ butternut squash, deseeded
45g (1½oz) dark chocolate (70% cocoa solids), roughly chopped
15g (½oz/1 tbsp) honey or maple syrup
2 tsp cocoa powder
2 eggs
105g (3½oz/½ cup) coconut sugar or dark muscovado (soft brown) sugar
pinch of sea salt
1 tsp vanilla extract
60g (2¼oz/⅔ cup) ground almonds
25g (1oz/¼ cup) buckwheat flour
½ tsp baking powder
1 tsp ground cinnamon
pinch of psyllium husk (optional)
edible gold dust, to decorate
rapeseed oil (canola), for greasing

Preheat the oven to 200°C/fan 180°C/400°F. Wrap the butternut squash in foil and roast for 40–45 minutes until tender. Remove from the oven and cool in the foil. Scrape the flesh from the skin and purée in a blender until fine. Weigh out 150g (5¼oz).

Place the chocolate and purée in a heatproof bowl and heat gently over a pan of simmering water or in the microwave until just warm and the chocolate has started to melt. Remove from the heat, stir and set aside to let the chocolate finish melting. Once completely melted, add the honey and cocoa and stir to mix well.

In a separate bowl, whisk the eggs, sugar salt and vanilla together on medium-high speed for 5 minutes until paler and doubled in volume.

In another bowl, sift together the ground almonds, flour, baking powder, cinnamon and ground psyllium (if using).

When the eggs are well whisked, gently fold through the butternut purée mixture until well blended. Add the dry ingredients and fold again until smooth. Leave for 10 minutes.

Preheat the oven to 180°C/fan 160°C/350°F and grease an 8-hole standard cupcake or oval silicone friand mould (each cavity dimensions about 7.5 x 5.5cm/3 x 2¼in) with a little rapeseed (canola) or coconut oil and place on a baking sheet. Fill the moulds with the batter to just below the top, then bake for 30 minutes, or until the tops spring back when pressed and the sponge feels soft to touch.

Cool the cakes still in the moulds on a wire rack for 20 minutes, before chilling until cold. De-mould the cakes when completely cold.

For the filling, process the dates with the remaining ingredients in a blender, scraping down the

ingredients and method continue overleaf

FOR THE SALTED CARAMEL FILLING

180g (6½oz/1⅓ cups) soft pitted
dates (ideally Medjool)
20g (¾oz/1½ tbsp) cashew
nut butter
20g (¾oz/1½ tbsp) coconut oil
20g (¾oz/1 tbsp plus 2 tsp) coconut
sugar or dark muscovado
(soft brown) sugar
¼ tsp sea salt
1 tsp vanilla paste or seeds from
½ vanilla pod (bean)

FOR THE CHOCOLATE CARAMEL GANACHE

150g (5¼oz) dark chocolate (55%
cocoa solids), roughly chopped
150g (5¼oz/½ cup) coconut cream
pinch of sea salt
1 tsp maple syrup

sides occasionally, until it is a
thick smooth paste.

Using a sharp knife, cut a small
hole in the middle of each cake
and fill with about 1 tsp of the
caramel. Set the rest of the
caramel aside.

For the ganache, place the
chocolate in a heatproof bowl.
Bring the remaining ingredients
to the boil in a pan, then pour
over the chocolate to cover
and leave for 1 minute to melt.
Gently stir the ganache until the
mixture just comes together and
looks shiny. Stir in the reserved
caramel. Cover directly with
clingfilm (plastic wrap) and cool
at room temperature until it is
the consistency of soft butter.

Whisk the ganache for 5
minutes, or until aerated and
thickened, then use it to fill
a piping bag fitted with your
choice of nozzle and pipe a ruffle
finish on top of each cake. Dust
with edible gold dust.

TIPS:

*If the dates are not soft and sticky, soak them in a heatproof bowl
of boiling water for 5 minutes before draining.*

This has to be one of my favourite cakes in the book. The subtle colour difference in the cake layers is really satisfying – like a homely rainbow cake, but with none of the artificial colours. If the coconut frosting seems a little too involved, feel free to replace with your usual frosting, dairy-free or not. (Pictured overleaf.)

Heritage Carrot Layer Cake

DF

MAKES A 15-CM (6-IN) CAKE
to serve 6–8

65g (2¼oz/½ cup) walnuts
160g (5¾oz/scant 1¼ cups) wholemeal (wholewheat) spelt flour
20g (¾oz/scant ¼ cup) cornflour (cornstarch) or tapioca flour
1½ tsp ground cinnamon
½ tsp ground nutmeg
1 tsp bicarbonate of soda (baking soda)
1 large yellow heritage carrot
1 large purple heritage carrot
1 large orange carrot
juice of ½ lemon
2 eggs (about 110g/4oz)
pinch of sea salt
250g (8¾oz/1⅓ cups) golden caster (granulated) sugar or demerara (raw brown) sugar
100g (3½fl oz/7 tbsp) rapeseed (canola) oil, plus extra for greasing
Candied Carrot Strips (see page 134), to decorate
handful of chopped walnuts, to decorate (optional)

Preheat the oven to 200°C/fan 180°C/400°F and toast the walnuts on a baking sheet for 5–6 minutes until lightly browned. Cool, then roughly chop.

Reduce the oven temperature to 180°C/fan 160°C/350°F. Grease the base and sides of 3 x 15-cm (6-in) sandwich tins with rapeseed (canola) oil and line the bases with a circle of baking parchment.

Sift together the flours, spices and bicarbonate of soda (baking soda) and set aside. Grate half of each carrot separately, using the finer cheese-grating part of a box grater, and weigh out 100g (3½oz) of each colour into 3 separate medium bowls. Top with a squeeze of lemon juice to prevent discoloration.

In a large mixing bowl, whisk together the eggs, salt and sugar until thick and doubled in volume. Keep whisking on a high speed, adding the oil gradually until incorporated. Gently fold through the dry ingredients, stopping before it looks completely smooth.

Top each of the bowls of grated carrot with 210g (7¼oz) of the cake batter and one-third of the chopped walnuts, and fold each through gently in turn. Fill each cake tin separately with the different coloured carrot cake batter and bake for 30 minutes, or until slightly browned, and the tops spring back when gently pressed.

Cool the cakes, still in their tins, until warm, then turn out onto a wire rack to cool completely. Chill until ready to layer with the frosting.

For the frosting, soften the creamed coconut either for a

ingredients and method continue on page 76

FOR THE LEMON COCONUT FROSTING

150g (5¼oz/½ cup plus 2 tbsp)
  creamed coconut
90g (3¼oz/½ cup) coconut oil
150g (5¼oz/½ cup) coconut cream
15g (½oz/1 tbsp) lemon juice
finely grated zest of 1 lemon
240g (8½oz/1¾ cups) golden icing
  (confectioners') sugar, sifted

minute or two in the microwave or in a heatproof bowl set over a pan of gently simmering water until it is a thick but stirrable consistency, then process in a blender until smooth. Add the coconut oil and process again. Scrape into a bowl and stir with a balloon whisk every few minutes until the mixture has cooled slightly and thickened, but not hardened. Add the coconut cream, lemon juice and zest and stir in until smooth.

Add the icing (confectioners') sugar and beat with a hand-held electric whisk for 2–3 minutes until smooth. If the mixture feels too soft to spread onto the cake, chill for 30 minutes and re-beat.

To assemble the cake, trim the tops of the sponges level. Place one of the sponges, crust side down, on a serving plate and spread with a layer of the frosting. Top with the next layer of sponge and spread with more frosting. Place the final layer on top, crust side up, and spread with a thin layer of frosting on top and on the sides. Chill for 30 minutes or longer to set.

Spread some clean, crumb-free frosting on top of the cake and spread out, then spread more frosting around the sides, scraping off the excess to give a clean finish. Run a palette knife around the sides horizontally to leave a rustic finish. Decorate the top with piped domes or swirls of frosting and some Candied Carrot Strips and chopped walnuts, if using.

Something as simple as an unusual mould can be enough to elevate a basic cake to superstar status. These super-moist and luscious chocolate beetroot domes are deceptively quick to make; even dipping them in the ganache glaze is quick and easy. Decorate with edible fresh or dried rose petals, or with the candied beetroot slices on page 135.

Chocolate Beetroot Domes

GF | WF | DF

MAKES 12 MINI-CAKES

225g (7¾oz) red or golden beetroot, cut into large chunks
65g (2¼oz) dark chocolate (55% cocoa solids), cut into rough chunks
20g (¾oz/1 tbsp) honey
1 tbsp cocoa powder
3 medium eggs
150g (5¼oz/¾ cup) rapadura or light muscovado (soft brown) sugar
large pinch of sea salt
90g (3¼oz/scant 1 cup) ground almonds
35g (1¼oz/¼ cup) buckwheat flour
¼ tsp bicarbonate of soda (baking soda)
¼ tsp ground psyllium husk (optional)
rapeseed (canola) or coconut oil, for greasing

Either steam the beetroot or microwave with 2 tbsp water for 10 minutes, or until just tender. Purée everything, including the water, until fine.

Add the chocolate to the warm purée and leave for a few minutes to melt. Add the honey and cocoa powder and blend again, until well mixed.

Place the eggs in a bowl, add the rapadura and salt and whisk on medium-high speed for 5 minutes until paler and doubled in volume.

In a separate bowl, sift together the ground almonds, flour, bicarbonate of soda (baking soda) and ground psyllium, if using.

When the eggs are well whisked, gently fold through the beetroot purée mixture until well blended. Use a lifting motion to keep the

mixing light and retain some of the air. Add the dry ingredients and fold again until smooth. Leave for 5–10 minutes.

Preheat the oven to 180°C/ fan 160°C/350°F. Grease 2 hemisphere silicone moulds, roughly 29.5 x 17cm (11¾ x 6½in) with a little rapeseed (canola) or coconut oil and place on a baking sheet. Scrape the rested batter into a jug and fill the moulds to just below the top.

Bake for 25–30 minutes, or until the tops spring back when gently pressed, but the sponge still feels soft to the touch.

Cool the cakes in the moulds on a wire rack for 20 minutes, before chilling in the fridge or freezer until cold. De-mould the cakes when completely cold, then chill.

ingredients and method continue on page 79

FOR THE CHOCOLATE GANACHE
60g (2¼oz/¼ cup) honey
small pinch of sea salt
250g (8¾oz) dark chocolate (55%
    cocoa solids), roughly chopped
1 tbsp coconut oil

TO DECORATE
edible dried petals, such as rose
    petals or cornflowers
Candied Beetroot Slices (see page
    135), optional

For the ganache, heat the honey in a small pan over a medium heat until it boils and caramelizes. This should only take a few minutes, so don't leave it unattended – the colour will darken and the honey will smell caramelized. Add 110g (4fl oz/½ cup) water and salt, and heat gently to dissolve the caramelized honey. Cool slightly.

Place the chocolate in a heatproof bowl, pour over the honey water to cover and leave for 1 minute to melt. Add the coconut oil and stir gently until smooth.

Dip the cakes top-down into the ganache. Lift out, shake off the excess and let them set on top of a wire rack. Top with edible dried petals and Candied Beetroot Slices, if making. Use a knife to lift the cakes from underneath when you want to move them onto a serving plate.

Autumnal and comforting, these nutty cookies are easy to make and great with a cup of tea or as a lunchbox treat. The cinnamon provides a spicy twist to balance the distinctive buckwheat flavour.

Buckwheat, Hazelnut & Cinnamon Shorties

WF | GF | DF | VG

MAKES ABOUT 16 COOKIES

105g (3½oz/generous ¾ cup) hazelnuts, unskinned
35g (1¼oz/heaping 2 tbsp) coconut oil
35g (1¼oz/heaping 2 tbsp) smooth peanut butter or hazelnut butter
10g (¼oz/2 tsp) maple syrup
3–4 tsp unsweetened almond milk
105g (3½oz/scant 1 cup) buckwheat flour
1½ tsp ground cinnamon
1 tsp ground flaxseed
pinch of sea salt
60g (2¼oz/5 tbsp) rapadura or light muscovado (soft brown) sugar

Preheat the oven to 200°C/ fan 180°C/400°F and toast the hazelnuts on a baking sheet until just browned, about 5–6 minutes. Remove from the oven and cool.

Melt the coconut oil and mix with the nut butter, maple syrup and 2 teaspoons of the almond milk until smooth. Cool.

Blend the hazelnuts with the buckwheat flour in a blender until it is a fine texture and just begins to clump. Add the cinnamon, ground flaxseed, salt and rapadura, and blend again until well mixed.

Transfer the mixture to a bowl, add the oil/peanut butter mixture and mix by hand or with a knife until the dough comes together. If needed, add an extra 1–2 teaspoons of almond milk to help bind. The dough should just be coming together and very slightly crumbly.

Form the dough into a log shape roughly 5cm (2in) across and wrap in foil or clingfilm (plastic wrap). Chill for 1 hour, or until firm or up to 3 days before baking.

Preheat the oven to 180°C/fan 160°C/350°F and line a baking sheet with baking parchment. Slice the log into approximately 1-cm (½-in) thick rounds, and space out 3cm (1¼in) apart on the baking sheet. Bake for 15 minutes, or until turning golden brown round the edges. Cool on the tray. Store at room temperature for up to 5 days.

This is a beautifully simple recipe; easy to make but disproportionately satisfying once baked. If you don't do that much baking, this is a great place to start. Always weigh out your mashed bananas, though, as too much or too little will make a big difference to the cake texture.

Banana Walnut Loaf

DF | VG

MAKES A SMALL LOAF
to serve 4–6

35g (1¼oz/¼ cup) walnuts
85g (3oz/⅔ cup) wholemeal (wholewheat) spelt flour
20g (¾oz/scant ¼ cup) cornflour (cornstarch) or tapioca flour
1 tsp ground cinnamon
¼ tsp ground nutmeg
⅓ tsp baking powder
⅓ tsp bicarbonate of soda (baking soda)
about 2 large ripe bananas, plus an extra half banana to decorate
pinch of sea salt
45g (1½fl oz/3 tbsp) rapeseed (canola) oil
80g (3oz/¼ cup) maple syrup
1 tsp cider vinegar
1 tsp vanilla paste
handful of demerara (raw brown) sugar to sprinkle
rapeseed (canola) oil, for greasing

Preheat the oven to 200°C/fan 180°C/400°F and toast the walnuts on a baking sheet for 5–6 minutes until lightly browned. Cool, then roughly chop.

Reduce the oven temperature to 180°C/fan 160°C/350°F and grease a 450-g (1-lb) loaf tin with a little rapeseed (canola) oil and line with baking parchment.

Sift together the flours with the spices and raising agents in a bowl.

Weigh the bananas. You need 165g (5¾oz) and mash well. Place the mashed bananas in a bowl and blend with the salt, oil, maple syrup, vinegar and vanilla with a balloon whisk. Tip in the dry ingredients and fold through with a spatula until just blended, then fold in the walnuts.

Scrape the mixture into the loaf tin, leaving it a little domed in the middle. Slice the extra half piece of banana lengthways and place this on top to decorate. Sprinkle with a little demerara (raw brown) sugar all over the top and bake for 45 minutes, or until the top is browned and springs back when pressed. An inserted cocktail stick should come out clean.

Let the cake cool in the tin until just warm, then turn out onto a wire rack to cool completely. Brush the bananas with a little extra maple syrup to add a little shine.

OK, so the name is a little tongue-in-cheek! But what else would you call a free-from version of millionaire's shortbread with date caramel and loads of nutritious ingredients like pecans, nut butter and rye flour? This is truly a modern version of the all-indulgent cookie, but unlike the traditional recipe, it won't leave you feeling sluggish and weighed-down afterwards.

Hipster Shortbread

WF | DF | VG

MAKES 12 MINI-SHORTBREADS

FOR THE BASE
90g (3¼oz/¾ cup) pecans
30g (1oz/2 tbsp) coconut oil
30g (1oz/2 tbsp) cashew nut butter
10g (¼oz/2 tsp) maple syrup
90g (3¼oz/¾ cup) wholegrain
　rye flour
2 large pinches of sea salt
50g (1¾oz/¼ cup) rapadura
　or light muscovado
　(soft brown) sugar
20g (¾oz/¼ cup) desiccated (dry
　unsweetened) coconut

FOR THE SALTED CARAMEL FILLING
245g (8½oz/scant 2 cups) soft
　pitted dates (ideally Medjool)
28g (1oz/2 tbsp) cashew nut butter
28g (1oz/2 tbsp) coconut oil
28g (1oz/2½ tbsp) coconut
　sugar or dark muscovado
　(soft brown) sugar
⅓ tsp sea salt
1½ tsp vanilla paste or seeds from
　½ vanilla pod (bean)

FOR THE CHOCOLATE TOPPING
150g (5¼oz) dark chocolate
　(70% or less cocoa solids),
　roughly chopped
10g (¼oz/2 tsp) coconut oil
small handful of desiccated coconut

Preheat the oven to 200°C/fan 180°C/400°F and toast the pecans on a baking sheet for 5–6 minutes until just browned. Cool. Reduce the oven temperature to 190°C/fan 170°C/375°F.

Melt the coconut oil and mix with the cashew nut butter and maple syrup until smooth. Cool.

Blend the pecans with the flour until it is a fine texture and just begins to clump. Add the salt and rapadura and blend again until well mixed. Transfer the mixture to a bowl and add the oil/cashew nut butter mixture. Combine until the mixture forms small clumps that just hold together when pressed. Mix in the desiccated coconut.

Divide the base evenly between the cavities of 2 x 6-hole square silicone moulds and press down with your fingertips. Place the mould on a baking sheet and bake for 15 minutes, or until the bases are just browning at the edges and looking dry. Cool.

For the filling, process the dates with the remaining ingredients in a blender, scraping down the sides occasionally, until it is a thick smooth paste. Either, scrape the mixture into a piping bag and pipe the filling onto the base, or spoon onto the base and use the back of a damp spoon to spread over evenly. Chill.

For the topping, place the chocolate and coconut oil in a heatproof bowl set over a pan of simmering water and melt gently, stirring occasionally. When melted, remove from the heat and stir thoroughly until combined. Pour over the top of the chilled caramel bases and tap the bottom of the baking sheet to even out the chocolate. Leave to set for 5 minutes at room temperature before sprinkling with a little desiccated coconut.

Chill for at least 30 minutes before de-moulding. Store in an airtight container at room temperature for up to 3 days.

This is a great 'free-from' dinner party pudding that looks much more complicated than it actually is. It uses a meringue-based French sponge that's very quick to make and works well as a gluten-free version.

Marquise au Chocolat

WF | GF | DF

SERVES 12–16

3 egg whites (about 100g/3½oz)
pinch of sea salt
80g (3oz/scant ½ cup) golden caster (superfine) sugar (or demerara sugar, finely ground)
30g (1oz/¼ cup) brown rice flour
40g (1½oz/scant ½ cup) ground almonds
30g (1oz/¼ cup) pistachios, roughly chopped, plus a few extra pistachios, roughly chopped, to decorate
coconut oil, for greasing

FOR THE GANACHE FILLING

200g (7oz/⅔ cup) coconut cream
20g (¾oz/2¼ tbsp) maple syrup
large pinch of sea salt
140g (5oz) dark chocolate (70% cocoa solids), roughly chopped
20g (¾oz/2 tsp) coconut oil

Preheat the oven to 190°C/fan 170°C/375°F. Grease a Swiss (jelly) roll tin or a shallow baking tin with a little coconut oil and line with baking parchment.

Whisk the egg whites with the salt until light and foamy; they should hold a firm peak. Sprinkle on one-quarter of the sugar and whisk for 20 seconds until incorporated, then add the next quarter of sugar and whisk again. Repeat with the remaining sugar, then whisk for a minute until the meringue is firm and glossy.

In a separate bowl, sift together the flour and ground almonds and gently fold into the meringue. Make sure there are no lumps. Scrape the mix into the tin and spread out as evenly as possible. Sprinkle with the chopped pistachios and bake for 12–15 minutes, or until it has puffed up, slightly browned and springs back when pressed. Cool in the tin on a wire rack.

For the filling, place all the ingredients in a heatproof

bowl set over a pan of gently simmering water and melt for 10 minutes, stirring occasionally. Remove from the heat and cool for 1 minute, then stir with a balloon whisk until the ganache is smooth. Cover the top directly with clingfilm (plastic wrap) and leave at room temperature until cooled, but still pliable.

To assemble, place the sponge upside down onto a fresh piece of baking parchment and peel off the backing paper. Trim the sponge at the edges and slice into 3 pieces that will fit snugly into a 900-g (2-lb) loaf tin. Line the base and sides of the tin with baking parchment.

Whisk the ganache until aerated and paler, but still spreadable. Working quickly, lay a piece of sponge on the bottom of the tin and top with one-third of the ganache. Spread out evenly, then top with the next piece of sponge. Repeat the process, finishing with a layer of ganache. Smooth the top and sprinkle with extra pistachios. Cover with clingfilm and chill until ready to serve.

I absolutely love chai lattes, and the great thing about adding spices to sweet treats is that the flavours are enhanced without the need for lots of sugar. I have chosen a combination of maple syrup and coconut sugar for sweetness, which gives these cheesecakes a warmer, more autumnal feel. And, of course, they are dairy-free, gluten-free and vegan so everyone can enjoy them!

Chai Latte Cheesecakes

WF | GF | DF | VG

MAKES 8 SMALL CHEESECAKES

1 quantity of Cheesecake Base
    (see page 131)
120g (4¼oz/1 cup) cashew nuts
pinch of salt
80g (3oz/5 tbsp) coconut oil
60g (2¼oz/scant ¼ cup) maple
    syrup
40g (1½oz/3¼ tbsp) coconut sugar
    or dark muscovado
    (soft brown) sugar
3 tsp cider vinegar
220g (7¾oz/¾ cup) coconut cream

FOR THE CHAI SPICE MIX

1 tsp ground black pepper
1 tsp ground nutmeg
2 tsp ground cardamom
2 tsp ground cloves
4 tsp ground cinnamon
4 tsp ground ginger

To make the chai spice, place all the ground spices in a small jam jar, seal with a lid and shake to mix well. Use as needed.

Make the Cheesecake Base according to the instructions on page 131, using an 8-hole round silicone mould (each about 5cm/2in diameter).

For the filling, soak the cashews in cold water for 1 hour. Drain and blend with the salt in a blender until as fine as possible. Add the coconut oil and blend again until completely smooth.

Add the maple syrup, coconut sugar, vinegar, coconut cream and 3½ teaspoons of chai spice mix and blend again until well mixed and smooth.

Use a jug or piping bag to fill the moulds evenly. Chill the cheesecakes in the fridge overnight before de-moulding and serving, or freeze for 2 or more hours. If frozen, they are easier to de-mould, but best left to soften in the fridge for an hour or two before serving. They will keep well in a covered container in the fridge for 2–3 days.

I developed this quick bread as a treat for my sister when, in addition to everything else, she had to cut out yeast. The large amount of ground flaxseed helps to keep the loaf moist for a few days, in contrast to many gluten-free loaves, which get stale and dry so quickly. It also contains plenty of fibre, protein and omega-3 fatty acids from the dates, teff, pecans and flaxseeds, so is a very nutritious snack.

Quick Date & Pecan Bread

WF | GF | DF

MAKES A SMALL LOAF
to serve 4–6

80g (3oz/¾ cup) pecans
100g (3½oz/¾ cup) soft pitted dates (ideally Medjool)
300g (10fl oz/1¼ cups) wholebean soya milk
1½ tsp cider vinegar
1 egg
½ tsp sea salt
2 tsp honey
115g (4oz/1 cup) rice flour
30g (1oz/¼ cup) brown teff flour
30g (1oz/scant ¼ cup) ground arrowroot
50g (1¾oz/½ cup) ground flaxseed
1 tsp ground psyllium
½ tsp bicarbonate of soda (baking soda)
1½ tsp baking powder
1 tsp ground cinnamon
rapeseed (canola) oil, for greasing

Cut a strip of baking parchment the same width as a 450-g (1-lb) loaf tin and long enough to reach up both sides. Grease and line the loaf tin with a little rapeseed (canola) oil and the piece of baking parchment, so that the base and 2 long sides are covered with a little overlap.

Reserve a few pecans and set aside. Preheat the oven to 200°C/fan 180°C/400°F and toast the remaining pecans on a baking sheet for 6 minutes, or until lightly browned. Cool, then chop roughly.

Add 20g (¾oz/⅛ cup) of the dates to the soya milk and vinegar, and process in a blender until smooth. Add the egg, salt and 1 teaspoon of the honey and process again. Chop the remaining dates finely.

Sift together the flours, arrowroot, flaxseed, psyllium, raising agents and cinnamon into a large bowl. Mix in the chopped pecans and dates, then add the liquid ingredients. Combine for 2–3 minutes with a rubber spatula until the mixture thickens.

Scrape the mixture into the loaf tin and rest in the tin for 15 minutes before baking. Warm the remaining honey in the microwave and mix in the reserved pecans until well coated. Top the loaf with the honeyed pecans and bake for 55 minutes, or until well browned and baked through.

Cool on a wire rack and de-mould the loaf while still warm. When cold, store wrapped in foil at room temperature for up to 3 days.

A totally non-optional treat for Thanksgiving, and autumn in general! My recipe is vegan-friendly and full of extra nutrients from the nuts, coconut oil, vinegar and fresh, not canned, pumpkin. I used some mini brioche moulds for these as I love the depth and shape for the pumpkin pie, but you can use regular 10-cm (4-in) shallow tartlet tins; in which case the recipe makes five pies.

Spiced Pumpkin Pies

WF | GF | DF | VG

MAKES 6 MINI PIES

1 quantity of Pastry (see page 130)
60g (2¼oz/½ cup) cashew nuts
250g (8¾oz) pumpkin or butternut squash
pinch of sea salt
50g (1¾oz/¼ cup) coconut oil, melted
55g (2oz/scant ¼ cup) maple syrup
1 tsp ground cinnamon
½ tsp ground ginger
¼ tsp ground nutmeg
large pinch of allspice
80g (3oz/¼ cup) coconut cream
½ tsp cider vinegar

Make the Pastry according to the instructions on page 130, using it to line 6 mini brioche tins, 6cm (2½in) in diameter.

Preheat the oven to 200°C/fan 180°C/400°F and put a baking sheet into the oven to heat. Line the bases of the moulds with baking parchment, then fill with rice or lentils. Gather the edges of the parchment together loosely in the centre and bake on the preheated tray for 20 minutes, or until the edges of the pastry are just beginning to brown. Remove the rice and cook the pastry cases for a further 3–4 minutes, or until the bases look dry. Cool in the tins on a wire rack until cold. Remove the tart cases from the tins before filling.

For the filling, soak the cashews in cold water for 1 hour.

Meanwhile, peel, deseed and dice the pumpkin, then steam over a pan or in a microwave with a little water until just tender. Cool, then purée and weigh out 130g (4½oz).

Drain the cashews and blend in a blender with the salt until as fine as possible. Add the coconut oil and blend again until completely smooth.

Add the maple syrup, spices, cooled pumpkin purée, coconut cream and vinegar, and blend again until well mixed and smooth. Divide evenly between the tart cases and chill for a few hours until set.

I love a classic red velvet cake with cream cheese frosting, but it's not exactly a healthy option! This recipe re-creates the same vanilla-cocoa flavour, but in a vegan version that includes all the goodness of beetroot, extra fibre from the wholegrain flours and flaxseeds, plus a lower sugar content. The frosting is a little more work than a standard recipe, but avoids having to turn to margarine or 'fake' cream cheese.

Beetroot Red Velvet Cake

DF | VG

MAKES A 20-CM (8-IN) CAKE
to serve 10–12

2 medium beetroots, cut into
   large chunks
2 tbsp ground flaxseed
90g (3fl oz/6 tbsp) rapeseed
   (canola) oil, plus extra for
   greasing
300g (10fl oz/1¼ cups) vegan
   yoghurt, such as soya or coconut
400g (14oz/2 cups) rapadura
   or light muscovado
   (soft brown) sugar
½ tsp sea salt
2 tbsp vanilla paste, or seeds from
   2 vanilla pods (beans)
30g (1oz/⅓ cup) cocoa powder
260g (9¼oz/2 cups) wholemeal
   (wholewheat) spelt flour
80g (3oz/⅔ cup) buckwheat flour
60g (2¼oz/⅔ cup) ground almonds
1½ tsp bicarbonate of soda
   (baking soda)
2 tbsp cider vinegar
Candied Beetroot Hearts (see page
   135), to decorate

Either steam the beetroot or microwave with 2 tablespoons of water for 10 minutes, or until just tender. Cool, then purée it all (including the water, if using) until smooth. Weigh out 200g/7oz purée.

Preheat the oven to 180°C/fan 160°C/350°F. Grease the base and sides of two 5 x 20-cm (2 x 8-in) cake tins with a little rapeseed (canola) oil and line the bases with a circle of baking parchment.

Mix the flaxseed with 6 tablespoons of warm water and leave for 10 minutes.

Using a balloon whisk, blend the flaxseed with the beetroot purée, the rapeseed oil, yoghurt, rapadura, salt, vanilla and cocoa powder in a mixing bowl until completely smooth.

Sift together the flours and ground almonds, then mix into the liquid ingredients with the balloon whisk until smooth.

In a small bowl, add the bicarbonate of soda (baking soda) to the vinegar and stir with a teaspoon. Add the foaming mix straight into the cake batter and gently fold together with the whisk. Take care not to overmix, or the batter will become tough.

Scrape the cake batter evenly between the tins and bake for 35–45 minutes, or until the tops spring back when gently pressed and an inserted cocktail stick comes out clean.

Cool the cakes, still in their tins, until just warm, then de-mould and cool on a wire rack until cold. Chill until ready to trim and frost.

ingredients and method continue overleaf

FOR THE VANILLA COCONUT FROSTING

300g (10½oz/1¼ cups) creamed
    coconut
180g (6½oz/1 cup) coconut oil
300g (10½oz/1¼ cup) coconut
    cream
30g (1fl oz/2 tbsp) lemon juice
1 tbsp vanilla paste or seeds of
    1 vanilla pod (bean)
480g (17oz/3½ cups) golden icing
    (confectioners') sugar, sifted

For the frosting, soften the creamed coconut either for a minute or two in the microwave or in a heatproof bowl set over a pan of gently simmering water, until it is a thick but stirrable consistency, then process in a blender until smooth. Add the coconut oil and process again. Scrape into a bowl and stir with a balloon whisk every few minutes until the mixture has cooled slightly and thickened, but not hardened. Add the coconut cream, lemon juice and vanilla and stir until smooth.

Add the icing (confectioners') sugar and beat with a hand-held electric whisk for 2–3 minutes until smooth. If the mixture feels too soft to spread onto the cake, chill for 30 minutes and re-beat.

To assemble the cake, trim the tops of the sponges level, then slice each sponge in half, so you have 4 layers in total. Place one of the sponges, crust side down, on a serving plate and spread with a layer of the frosting. Top with the next layer of sponge and spread with more frosting.

Repeat until you reach the final layer, placing it crust side up, and spread with a thin layer of frosting on the top and on the sides. Chill for 30 minutes or longer to set.

Spread some clean, crumb-free frosting on top of the cake and spread out, then spread more frosting around the sides, scraping off the excess to give a clean finish. Chill again for about 30 minutes to firm, then decorate the sides with Candied Beetroot Hearts, wiping off any excess syrup and sticking directly onto the frosting. The top can also be decorated with piped swirls of leftover frosting and dried beetroot hearts.

The flavour profile of coconut sugar is ideal for sticky toffee – caramel, deep and complex. The dates naturally add sweetness and stickiness, while the sweet potato provides moisture, helping to create a vegan, high-fibre, nutritious version of this dessert that still tastes super-indulgent!

Sticky Toffee Pudding with Toffee Sauce

DF | GF | WF | VG

SERVES 6

1 small sweet potato
40g (1½oz/⅓ cup) pecans
145g (5fl oz/⅔ cup) strong Earl Grey tea
145g (5oz/1 cup) soft pitted dates (ideally Medjool), chopped
1 tbsp ground flaxseed
1 tbsp vanilla paste or 1 vanilla pod (bean), split in half lengthways and seeds scraped out
150g (5¼oz/¾ cup) coconut sugar or dark muscovado (soft brown) sugar
40g (1½oz/scant ¼ cup) coconut oil, melted
2 tsp cider vinegar
30g (1oz/2 tbsp) date syrup or black treacle (blackstrap molasses)
pinch of sea salt
50g (1¾oz/scant ½ cup) teff flour
25g (1oz/scant ¼ cup) buckwheat flour
75g (2¾oz/½ cup) rice flour
50g (1¾oz/½ cup) ground almonds
1 tsp bicarbonate of soda (baking soda)
1 quantity of Vegan Custard (see page 132; optional)

Preheat the oven to 200°C/fan 180°C/400°F. Roast the sweet potato on a baking sheet for 45 minutes, or until soft in the centre. Alternatively, microwave it for 8–10 minutes until soft. Cool, then scoop out and weigh 80g (3oz) of the flesh. Purée until smooth in a blender. Meanwhile, toast the pecans on a baking sheet for 5–6 minutes until lightly browned. Cool, then roughly chop.

Reduce the oven temperature to 180°C/fan 160°F/350°F and grease 6 individual pudding moulds or a small rectangular tin, about 20 x 15cm (8 x 6in) generously with coconut oil, or grease and line the tin with baking parchment.

Pour the tea over the dates in a bowl, cover and leave to soak for 20 minutes.

Place the flaxseed in another bowl and add 3 tablespoons of warm water. Mix well and leave for 10 minutes to thicken.

Lightly mash the soaked dates, so they are half puréed, half chunky. Add the sweet potato purée, vanilla, coconut sugar, coconut oil, vinegar, date syrup, flaxseed and salt and mix well.

In a separate bowl, sift together the flours, ground almonds and bicarbonate of soda (baking soda), then add to the wet ingredients with the pecans and mix well. Divide the batter between the moulds or fill the tin and leave for 10 minutes. Bake for 50 minutes, or until the sponge springs back when pressed. If the tops of the sponges get a little dark, cover with foil or reduce the oven temperature by 10°C/20°F.

ingredients and method continue overleaf

FOR THE STICKY TOFFEE SAUCE

65g (2¼oz/¼ cup) date syrup
100g (3½oz/½ cup) coconut
   sugar or dark muscovado
   (soft brown) sugar
120g (3½oz/scant ½ cup)
   coconut cream
30g (1oz/2 tbsp) coconut oil
45g (1½oz/2¼ tbsp) maple syrup
large pinch of sea salt
1 empty vanilla pod (if used in
   pudding), or 2 tsp vanilla paste

Let the puddings cool until just warm, then de-mould onto a baking sheet lined with baking parchment. Wrap in foil and store in the fridge until ready to heat.

For the sauce, gently simmer all the ingredients together in a pan for 10 minutes to thicken. If using vanilla paste, add this at the end of simmering. Chill until needed (it will keep for up to a week) and reheat gently before using.

Make the Vegan Custard according to the instructions on page 132, if using.

When ready to assemble, preheat the oven to 180°C/fan 160°C/350°F and place a tray of hot water at the bottom. Heat the puddings for 15 minutes, or until warmed through. Pour the hot sauce over and serve with custard or ice cream.

These are a great autumnal bake, and look really pretty in the mini bundt moulds. Any kind of squash can be used in place of the pumpkin, so feel free to change it according to the season and availability. They are very easy to make and are full of nutrients and protein from the flaxseed, hazelnuts and pumpkin, making for a super-wholesome bake.

Pumpkin, Khorasan & Chai Bundt Cakes

DF | VG

MAKES 12 MINI BUNDT CAKES

about ¼ small pumpkin
1 tbsp ground flaxseed
185g (6½oz/scant 1 cup) coconut sugar or dark muscovado (soft brown) sugar
65g (2¼oz/⅓ cup) coconut oil, melted, plus extra for greasing
1 tsp cider vinegar
60g (2fl oz/¼ cup) orange juice
pinch of sea salt
170g (6oz/1½ cups) khorasan (Kamut®) flour
40g (1½oz/¼ cup) ground hazelnuts, either ready-ground or toasted and ground in a blender
¼ tsp bicarbonate of soda (baking soda)
1 tsp baking powder
2½ tsp Chai Spice Mix (see page 88)

Preheat the oven to 200°C/fan 180°C/400°F. Wrap the pumpkin in foil and roast for 40–45 minutes until tender. Cool in the foil, then scrape the flesh from the skin and purée in a blender until smooth. Weigh out 180g (6½oz) into a bowl.

Reduce the oven temperature to 180°C/fan 160°C/350°F. Grease 2 x 6-hole silicone bundt moulds with a little coconut oil and place on a baking sheet.

Place the flaxseed in another bowl and add 3 tablespoons of warm water. Mix well and leave for 10 minutes to thicken.

Add the flaxseed to the pumpkin purée along with the coconut sugar, coconut oil, vinegar, orange juice and salt and mix well with a balloon whisk.

In a separate bowl, sift together the flour, ground hazelnuts, raising agents and spice mix. Add this to the wet ingredients and fold through gently with the whisk until just blended.

Pour or pipe the mixture into the moulds until it reaches just below the top and bake for 30 minutes, or until risen and golden in colour. Let the cakes rest in the moulds for 5 minutes, then turn upside down to de-mould. Cool on a wire rack until completely cold. These will keep well in an airtight container for 2–3 days.

Dark
+ SPICY

I love the combination of chocolate, citrus and spices in general, and this recipe is a great way to update your chocolate tart repertoire. The filling is incredibly easy to make, and if you don't have the time to make pastry you can always just double the filling quantities and serve it set in little espresso cups instead – in which case call them Mayan Chocolate Orange Pots!

Chocolate Orange Tarts with Mayan Spices

WF | GF | DF | VG

MAKES UP TO 10 SMALL TARTS

1 quantity of Pastry (see page 130)
Candied Orange Strips (see page 133), to decorate

FOR THE CHOCOLATE GANACHE FILLING

150g (5¼oz/½ cup) coconut cream
210g (7¼oz) dark chocolate (55% cocoa solids), roughly chopped
2 tsp maple syrup or brown rice syrup
pinch of sea salt
finely grated zest of 1 orange
¼ tsp chilli oil
½ tsp ground cinnamon
pinch of ground allspice

Make the Pastry according to the instructions on page 130, using it to line up to 10 x 8.5cm (3¼in) mini tart tins.

Preheat the oven to 200°C/fan 180°C/400°F and put a baking sheet into the oven to heat. Line the bases of the tart tins with baking parchment, then fill with rice or lentils. Gather the edges of the parchment together loosely in the centre and bake on the tray for 15 minutes, or until the edges of the pastry are just beginning to brown. Remove the rice and cook the pastry cases for a further 3–4 minutes, or until the bases look dry. Cool in the tins on a wire rack until cold. Remove the tart cases from the tins before filling.

For the filling, place all the ingredients into a heatproof bowl set over a pan of gently simmering water and melt for 10 minutes, stirring occasionally. Remove the bowl

from the pan and cool for 1 minute, then stir with a balloon whisk until the ganache is smooth.

Transfer the ganache to a jug and pour into the tart cases. Chill for at least 1 hour to firm up. Bring back to room temperature for 20 minutes before serving, and decorate with Candied Orange Strips on top.

The first time I gave some of this cake to a friend to try, he said it reminded him of the Yorkshire cake Parkin. He is very cautious about 'healthy' cakes, so after he finished several slices, I knew this would be a winner! It works very well baked in loaf tins too – in which case you will need to reduce the baking time a little.

Spiced Caramel Bundt cake

WF | GF | DF

MAKES A LARGE BUNDT CAKE
to serve 12–14

2 large sweet potatoes
240g (8½oz/1 cup) dairy-free yoghurt
4 eggs and 4 yolks
200g (7oz/1 cup) coconut sugar or dark muscovado (soft brown) sugar
200g (7oz/¾ cup) honey or maple syrup, plus extra for drizzling
40g (1½fl oz/3 tbsp) rapeseed (canola) oil
50g (1¾oz/scant ½ cup) buckwheat flour
230g (8oz/scant 1 cups) rice flour
40g (1½oz/⅓ cup) tapioca flour
4 tsp baking powder
1 tsp bicarbonate of soda (baking soda)
1½ tsp ground cinnamon
¼ tsp ground black pepper
½ tsp ground cardamom
coconut oil, for greasing

FOR THE ICING
240g (8½oz/1¾ cups) golden icing (confectioners') sugar
1 tbsp honey or maple syrup, plus extra 75g (2¾oz/¼ cup), for topping (optional)
juice of ½ orange

Preheat the oven to 200°C/ fan 180°C/400°F. Roast the sweet potatoes in foil for 45–50 minutes until tender inside and just starting to caramelize on the outside. Cool. Grease a bundt tin, about 25cm (10in) across thoroughly with coconut oil. Chill.

Scoop the cooled flesh from the sweet potatoes and blend until smooth. Weigh out 300g (10½oz) into a large bowl, then top with the yoghurt and blend well.

Whisk the eggs, yolks and coconut sugar for 4–5 minutes until thick and foamy. Gradually drizzle in the honey followed by the oil, while whisking on high speed. Add the potato-yoghurt mix and whisk in gently.

In a separate bowl, sift together all the dry ingredients. Fold the dry ingredients into the wet ingredients until well blended. Scrape the cake mix into the tin and leave to rest for 15 minutes.

Reduce the oven temperature to 180°C/fan 160°C/350°F.

Bake for 1 hour, or until well risen, springs back when pressed and an inserted cocktail stick comes out clean. Cool the cake in the tin until just warm, then de-mould carefully by flipping upside down onto a wire rack and removing the tin. Cool completely on the wire rack.

For the icing, sift the icing (confectioners') sugar into a bowl, add the honey or syrup and add enough orange juice to form a glacé icing the thickness of double (heavy) cream.

Pour the icing over the cooled cake and leave for a few minutes. Boil the extra honey or syrup, if using, on the hob or in the microwave for a minute to thicken, cool, then drizzle on top to finish.

A slightly more delicate, but still indulgent, version of a fondant, this pudding has the added bonus of the antioxidants, fibre, vitamins and minerals from the aubergine (eggplant) plus healthy fats from the nuts and chocolate. Crème fraîche is the perfect accompaniment as the sourness cuts through the rich chocolate, but if you are going non-dairy then try the coconut crème fraîche recipe below.

Chocolate Aubergine Fondant

WF | GF | DF

SERVES 4

1 medium aubergine (eggplant)
140g (5oz) dark chocolate (55% cocoa solids), roughly chopped, plus 40g (1½oz) extra chocolate for the centre
90g (3¼oz/scant ⅓ cup) honey
¼ tsp salt
1 egg and 1 yolk
50g (1¾oz/½ cup) ground almonds
1 tbsp cocoa powder
1 tsp baking powder
coconut oil, for greasing

FOR THE COCONUT CRÈME FRAÎCHE (OPTIONAL)

150g (5¼oz/½ cup) coconut cream
125g (4¼oz/½ cup) dairy-free yoghurt, such as soya or coconut
10g (¼oz/2 tsp) coconut oil, melted
juice of ¼ lemon

If making the coconut crème fraîche, mix all ingredients together with a small whisk, then chill for 2 days to sour and thicken.

Grease 4 medium ramekins with a generous amount of coconut oil and chill.

Pierce the aubergine (eggplant) all over and microwave on full power for 8–10 minutes, turning over halfway through, until completely soft inside. Alternatively, roast whole in a hot oven (200°C/fan 170°C/400°F) for 40 minutes. Cool slightly, then slice in half and scoop out the flesh. Weigh out 100g (3½oz) and purée in a blender. Add the 140g (5oz) chocolate on top and allow to melt for a few minutes. Add the honey and salt, and purée until smooth.

Scrape the mixture into a bowl, add the egg and yolk and whisk together with a balloon whisk. In a separate bowl, sift the ground

almonds, cocoa powder and baking powder, then add to the cake mix. Gently whisk together.

Use a jug or piping bag to fill the ramekins with the mix, pressing 1–2 squares of the extra chocolate into the centre of each. Chill the fondants for a few hours, or up to 2 days.

When ready to bake, preheat the oven to 200°C/ fan 170°C/400°F. Place the fondants on a baking sheet and bake in the centre of the oven for 15–18 minutes, or until just puffing up and looking baked on top. They will still be quite delicate with squidgy, runny centres.

Serve with fresh berries and the coconut crème fraîche.

Khorasan, also known as Kamut® flour, is an ancient wheat variety with a distinctive buttery flavour that works incredibly well with the spices and cashews here. It is nutritionally superior to common wheat in protein and trace minerals, but is not gluten-free, so if you have an intolerance then do avoid it.

Chai & Cashew Shortbread

DF | VG

MAKES 12 SLICES

90g (3¼oz/¾ cup) cashew nuts
20g (¾oz/1½ tbsp) coconut oil
30g (1oz/1 tbsp) cashew nut butter
20g (¾oz/2 tbsp) maple syrup
3–4 tsp unsweetened almond milk
110g (4oz/¾ cup) khorasan (Kamut®) flour
1½ tsp Chai Spice Mix (see page 88)
pinch of sea salt
50g (1¾oz/¼ cup) golden caster (granulated) sugar or demerara, (raw brown) ground fine

Preheat the oven to 200°C/ fan 180°C/400°F and toast the cashews on a baking sheet for 5–6 minutes until just browned. Cool.

Melt the coconut oil and mix with the nut butter, maple syrup and 2 teaspoons of the almond milk in a bowl, until smooth. Cool.

Blend the cashews with the flour in a blender until it is a fine texture and just begins to clump. Add the spices, salt and sugar and blend again until well mixed. Transfer the mixture to a bowl and add the oil/nut butter mixture. Mix by hand or with a knife until the dough comes together, adding an extra 1–2 teaspoons of almond milk to help bind. The dough should just be coming together and be very slightly crumbly.

Form the dough into a block roughly 1¼ x 2.5cm (3 x 1in) and wrap in foil or clingfilm (plastic wrap). Chill for 1 hour, or until firm, or for up to 3 days before baking.

Preheat the oven to 180°C/ fan 160°C/350°F and line a baking sheet with baking parchment. Trim the edges of the dough to neaten, then slice into 5-mm (¼-in) thick rectangles. Space them out 3cm (1¼in) apart on the tray and bake for 12–13 minutes, or until golden brown at the edges. Cool on the tray. Store at room temperature in a sealed container for up to 5 days.

This is a perfect winter masterpiece: blood oranges are quite tart and clementines slightly sweeter so the two balance each other ideally. It uses the whole fruit, so nothing is wasted and all the nutrients are included.

Spiced Blood Orange & Clementine Cake

WF | GF | DF

MAKES ONE 20-CM (8-IN) SQUARE LAYERED CAKE
to serve 10–12

1 blood orange, roughly chopped and pips removed
2 clementines, roughly chopped and pips removed
350g (12¼oz/3½ cups) ground almonds
3 tbsp rice flour
2 tsp cornflour (cornstarch)
2 tsp ground cinnamon
½ tsp ground allspice
1 tsp ground nutmeg
3 tsp baking powder
8 eggs
350g (12¼oz/2 cups) golden caster (granulated) sugar
rapeseed (canola) oil, for greasing

FOR THE CHOCOLATE GANACHE WITH MULLED WINE SPICES
75g (2¾oz/¼ cup) honey
pinch of sea salt
2 sachets of mulled wine spices
375g (13¼oz) dark chocolate (55% cocoa solids), roughly chopped
1½ tbsp coconut oil

TO DECORATE
Candied Blood Orange Crisps (see page 134)
edible gold dust

Place the fruit in a pan with enough water to just cover. Add a lid and cook for 45 minutes, or until the fruit is soft. Uncover and cook over a low heat until almost all but 2 tbsp of the liquid has evaporated. Cool, then blitz in a blender until it forms a fine purée. Weigh out 490g (17¼oz).

Sift together the ground almonds, flours, spices and baking powder.

Whisk the eggs and sugar for 1–2 minutes until just thick and foamy. Whisk in the fruit purée, then fold through the dry ingredients, allowing the mixture to deflate by half. Rest for 1 hour before baking.

Preheat the oven to 170°C/fan 150°C/340°F. Grease a 20-cm (8-in) square tin with rapeseed (canola) oil and line with baking parchment. Fill with one-third of the mix (about 560g/1¼lb). Bake for 35 minutes until browned and cooked through.

Cool completely on a wire rack before de-moulding. Wipe out the tin, fill with the next third of the cake mix and bake in the same way. If you have more than one tin, you can bake 2 or 3 at a time. Once all the cake layers are baked, wrap and chill.

For the ganache, bring the honey, 165g (5fl oz/⅔ cup) water, the salt and spice sachets to the boil in a pan. Remove from the heat and infuse for 1 hour. Heat again just to boiling point, then remove the sachets.

Place the chocolate in a heatproof bowl and pour over the honey mix to cover. Leave for 1 minute to melt. Add the coconut oil and stir gently with a balloon whisk until smooth. Cover the top directly with clingfilm (plastic wrap) and leave for 2–3 hours at room temperature until it is a pipeable consistency.

To assemble, trim the edges of the sponge to straighten. Place one of the sponges on a serving plate. Put the ganache into a piping bag fitted with a 1-cm (½-in) round nozzle and pipe peaks over the top. Place the next sponge on top and press down gently. Pipe ganache over the next layer in the same way, then repeat the process. Decorate with Candied Blood Orange Crisps and edible gold dust.

These little tarts are very nutrient-rich, as well as tasting like a fabulous treat! They are equally beautiful topped with a sprinkling of crushed Himalayan salt or, for a special occasion, some edible gold leaf.

Salted Caramel & Chocolate Tart

WF | GF | DF | VG

MAKES 5 SMALL TARTS

1 quantity of Pastry (see page 130)

FOR THE SALTED CARAMEL FILLING

180g (6½oz/1⅓ cups) soft pitted dates (ideally Medjool)
20g (¾oz/1½ tbsp) cashew nut butter
20g (¾oz/1½ tbsp) coconut oil
20g (¾oz/1 tbsp plus 2 tsp) coconut sugar or dark muscovado (soft brown) sugar
¼ tsp sea salt
1 tsp vanilla paste or seeds from ½ vanilla pod (bean)

FOR THE CHOCOLATE GANACHE TOPPING

100g (3½oz/⅓ cup) coconut cream
140g (5oz) dark chocolate (55% cocoa solids), roughly chopped
1 tsp brown rice syrup
pinch of sea salt
edible gold leaf, to decorate

Make the Pastry according to the instructions on page 130, using it line 5 x 10cm (4in) individual tart tins.

Preheat the oven to 200°C/fan 180°C/400°F and put a tray into the oven. Line the tart bases with baking parchment, then fill with rice or lentils. Gather the edges of the parchment together loosely in the centre and bake on the tray for 20 minutes, or until the edges of the pastry are just beginning to brown. Remove the rice and cook the pastry cases for a further 3–4 minutes, or until the bases look dry. Cool in the tins on a wire rack until cold. Remove the tart cases from the tins before filling

For the filling, process the dates with the remaining ingredients in a blender, scraping down the sides occasionally, until it is a thick smooth paste. Either scrape the mixture into a piping bag and pipe the filling onto the base of the baked tart case(s), or spoon onto the bottom and use the back of a damp spoon to spread evenly.

For the topping, place all the ingredients in a heatproof bowl set over a pan of gently simmering water and melt for 10 minutes, stirring occasionally. Cool for 1 minute. Stir with a balloon whisk until the ganache is smooth, then cool to room temperature before piping over the caramel-filled tart(s). Chill for at least 1 hour until firm. Bring back to room temperature for 20 minutes before serving with a little edible gold leaf for decoration.

Dark and slightly bitter, these are cookies for adults! The cocoa nibs will also give you a nice little caffeine kick – perfect for a mid-afternoon slump.

Rye Cocoa-nut Cookies

WF | DF | VG

MAKES 8–10 COOKIES

90g (3¼oz/generous ¾ cup) dark rye flour
90g (3¼oz/¾ cup) cocoa nibs
60g (2¼oz/5 tbsp) coconut sugar or dark muscovado (soft brown) sugar
45g (1½oz/3 tbsp) coconut oil
30g (1oz/2 tbsp) unsweetened cashew or almond butter
25g (1oz/2 tbsp) maple syrup
15g (½oz/scant ¼ cup) desiccated (dry unsweetened) coconut
3 tbsp unsweetened almond milk

TO FINISH

about 100g (3½oz) dark chocolate (70% cocoa solids), roughly chopped
about 50g (1¾oz/⅔ cup) desiccated coconut

Blend the flour with the cocoa nibs in a blender until fine. Add the sugar and blend again. Melt the coconut oil and mix with the nut butter and maple syrup. Cool slightly, then add to the flour mix in the blender. Pulse to blend until the mixture clumps together. Tip out into a bowl and add the desiccated (dry unsweetened) coconut. Work this in with your fingertips, then add the almond milk and bring the dough together into a ball.

Shape the dough into a log about 4cm (1½in) across, wrap in clingfilm (plastic wrap) or foil and chill for a few hours until firm.

Preheat the oven to 180°C/fan 160°C/350°F and line a baking sheet with baking parchment. Slice the log into 1-cm (½-in) rounds and place 3cm (1¼in) apart on the tray. Bake for 15 minutes, or until baked through, but not overly browned. Cool on a wire rack.

To finish, melt the chocolate gently in the microwave for 1 minute at a time, or in a heatproof bowl set over a pan of gently simmering water. Dip the bottom half of each cookie into the chocolate so it comes up halfway, then into the desiccated coconut. Allow to set on baking parchment. Store in an airtight container at room temperature for up to 5 days.

Don't be put off by the long ingredients list – weighing everything out is the most challenging part of the recipe; making it is child's play! I love the gentle warmth of the chilli and the underlying spiciness behind the chocolate. However, the spices and chilli are optional and can be adjusted or omitted as you wish.

Spicy Vegan Chocolate Cake

WF | GF | DF | VG

MAKES A 15-CM (6-IN) CAKE
to serve 6–8

FOR THE WET MIX
4 tsp ground flaxseed
100g (3½oz) dark chocolate (70% cocoa solids), roughly chopped
105g (3½oz/½ cup) coconut oil, melted, plus extra for greasing
40g (1½oz/3 tbsp) cashew nut butter or nut butter of choice
2 tsp chilli oil
420g (14¾oz/scant 2 cups) dairy-free yoghurt
1 tsp cider vinegar
275g (9¾oz/1½ cups minus 2 tbsp) coconut sugar or dark muscovado (soft brown) sugar
¼ tsp sea salt

FOR THE DRY MIX
130g (4½oz/1 cup) teff flour
50g (1¾oz/⅓ cup) brown rice flour
25g (1oz/¼ cup) cornflour (cornstarch) or tapioca flour
70g (2½oz/¾ cup) ground almonds
45g (1½oz/½ cup) cocoa powder
1½ tsp bicarbonate of soda (baking soda)
½ tsp xanthan gum (optional)
3 tsp Chai Spice Mix (see page 88)

For the ganache (see overleaf), place the chocolate in a heatproof bowl set over a pan of barely simmering water and warm until melted. Set aside.

Place all the remaining ganache ingredients in a pan and bring gradually to the boil, stirring occasionally. Once boiling, remove from the heat and scrape in the melted chocolate. Stir very gently once to make sure the chocolate is covered, then let melt for 1 minute. Stir with a spatula, then use a hand-held blender to blend until smooth. Transfer to a bowl, cover the top directly with clingfilm (plastic wrap) and leave at room temperature for several hours or overnight until a spreadable consistency.

For the cake, grease 4 x 15-cm (6-in) round sandwich tins with coconut oil and line with baking parchment.

Blend the ground flaxseed with 4 tablespoons of warm water and allow to thicken for 10 minutes.

Place the chocolate in a heatproof bowl, cover with ground flaxseed with 3 tablespoons of boiling water and the warm coconut oil and leave until melted. Stir the chocolate mixture together, then add the remaining wet mix ingredients, including the soaked flaxseed, and stir with a whisk to combine.

Sift together all the dry ingredients into a large bowl, add the wet mix and blend together using a balloon whisk. Divide the mixture evenly between the tins and level the tops. Leave for 10 minutes.

Preheat the oven to 180°C/fan 160°C/350°F.

Bake for 30 minutes, or until the tops spring back when

ingredients and method continue overleaf

FOR THE COCONUT CHOCOLATE GANACHE

500g (1lb 2oz) dark chocolate
 (ideally 55% cocoa solids),
 finely chopped
275g (9¾oz/scant 1 cup) coconut
 cream
65g (2¼oz/scant ¼ cup) brown
 rice syrup
large pinch of sea salt
35g (1¼oz/2 tbsp) coconut oil

TO DECORATE

chocolate shavings
edible gold dust
1 red chilli

gently pressed, but still feels soft. Cool the cakes still in the tins until just warm, then de-mould onto a wire rack to finish cooling completely. Chill before assembling.

Trim the tops of the cakes so they are just level. Place the first sponge on a serving plate, spread a thin layer of ganache (4–5mm/⅙–⅛in) on top, letting it overlap the sides slightly, then place the next sponge on top and press down gently. Spread another thin layer of ganache, repeat with the thir sponge, then top with the final layer of sponge, placing with the bottom crust side up. Spread the top and sides with more ganache. Chill for at least 30 minutes, then spread the top and sides of the cake with the

remaining ganache. Finish by removing any excess at the top with a palette knife, pulling the ganache towards the middle of the cake.

Chill until the ganache has set, then decorate with chocolate shavings, edible gold dust and a chilli.

TIP:

You can buy chilli-infused olive oil from most supermarkets. but to make your own. simply mix in 1 tbsp dried chilli flakes into a jam jar of rapeseed or olive oil and allow to infuse for several days before using. Over time the heat will increase so top up with more oil when you use some.

Fruit cake, GOOD fruit cake, is ideal afternoon-tea food for cold weather. I like mine with more interesting, varied dried fruits, but it can still be incredibly high in sugars and very rich. This recipe cuts through the intensity of a traditional cake by including grated fruit and vegetables, which serve to add moisture, bulk and some nutritional plus points. I have also swapped the butter for a small portion of coconut oil and included a variety of wholegrain flours for extra nutrients and fibre. The goji berries also add a great antioxidant boost, as well as a bright red seasonal burst of colour!

Christmas Fruit & Root Cake with Candied Fruit & Glazed Nuts

WF | GF | DF

MAKES A 15-CM (6-IN) CAKE
to serve 6–8

50g (1¾oz/3½ tbsp) coconut oil
125g (4¼oz/⅔ cup minus 2 tsp) coconut sugar or dark muscovado (soft brown) sugar
1 carrot
⅛ swede (rutabaga)
1 Bramley or cooking apple
2 eggs
Candied Kumquats (see page 135), to decorate

FOR THE FRUIT MIX
390g (13¾oz) mixed fruit
100g (3½oz/¾ cup) mixed peel
25g (1oz/¼ cup) goji berries
75g (2¾oz/½ cup) raisins
140g (5oz/1 cup) sultanas (golden raisins)
50g (1¾oz/⅓ cup) currants
50g (1¾oz/⅓ cup) dried apricots
finely grated zest of 1 orange
finely grated zest of 1 lemon
25g (1oz/⅓ cup) flaked (slivered) almonds
65g (2fl oz/¼ cup) spiced rum
juice of ½ orange

The day before baking (or several days before, if you're organized!), place all the ingredients for the fruit mix in a bowl, stir well and cover with clingfilm (plastic wrap). Leave overnight at room temperature.

The next day, heat the fruit mix in a large pan with the coconut oil and coconut sugar. When they are melted and almost steaming, cover and allow to cool.

Preheat the oven to 160°C/140°C (fan)/325°F. Grease a 15-cm (6-in) cake tin with coconut oil and line with a triple thickness of greaseproof paper or baking parchment. Insulate the sides with a layer of cardboard or newspaper, securing with string.

Peel and grate the carrot coarsely, then weigh out 50g (1¾oz). Do the same with the swede (rutabaga) and weigh out 50g (1¾oz), then the apple and weigh out 65g (2¼oz).

Tip the cooled dried fruit mixture into a large bowl. Add the eggs, and mix well. Add the grated vegetables and apple on top and mix again.

In a separate bowl, sift together all the dry ingredients and fold into the cake batter. Fill the tin, making sure to smooth down evenly. Tap the tin firmly to even out the batter, then leave a slight dip in the centre with the back of a spoon.

Bake in the middle of the oven for 2½ hours, or until baked

ingredients and method continue overleaf

Christmas Fruit & Root Cake continued

FOR THE DRY INGREDIENTS

50g (1¾oz/scant ½ cup) teff flour
25g (1oz/generous ⅛ cup) brown
   rice flour
15g (½oz/⅛ cup) buckwheat flour
1 tsp ground flaxseed
40g (1½oz/scant ½ cup) ground
   almonds
½ tsp baking powder
½ tsp ground cinnamon
¼ tsp ground ginger
¼ tsp ground nutmeg
⅛ tsp ground allspice

TO FINISH

340g (12oz) jar apricot jam
about 150g (5¼oz/1¼ cups) mixed
   nuts, such as brazils, almonds,
   pecans, etc.
about 100g (3½oz) candied fruit,
   such as kumquats (see page
   135), orange slices (see page
   133), lemon slices, glacé cherries

through, springing back when pressed and an inserted cocktail stick should come out clean. If the cake starts to brown too much during baking, cover the top with foil.

Leave the cake in the tin for 20 minutes, then brush with 2 tablespoons of extra spiced rum. Cool completely in the tin before de-moulding and wrapping in baking parchment and foil.

To finish, heat the jam until boiling, then strain to remove any pulp. Brush the jam over the top of the cake, then stick a selection of fruit and nuts on top. Brush extra warm apricot jam on top to glaze.

TIP:

The undecorated cake will keep well at a cool room temperature for up to 2 months.

These make a special warming, lightly spiced breakfast treat. The rye and buckwheat deliver plenty of fibre and complex carbs to see you through the morning, and with protein from the egg and nuts, as well as nutrients from the fruit, these are about as complete nutritionally as you can get from a muffin! If you feel like increasing the sweetness, top with a little extra demerara sugar before baking – it will give them a lovely crunch as well.

Rye, Buckwheat & Winter Fruit Muffins

WF | DF

MAKES 9 MUFFINS

70g (2½oz/½ cup) walnuts, roughly chopped (optional)
140g (5oz/generous ½ cup) unsweetened almond milk
1 tsp cider vinegar
100g (3½oz/scant 1 cup) dark rye flour
55g (2oz/½ cup) buckwheat flour
1½ tsp mixed spices of your choice (I used 1 tsp ground cinnamon and ¼ tsp each of ground nutmeg and allspice)
1¾ tsp baking powder
½ tsp bicarbonate of soda (baking soda)
1 firm Conference pear
1 Cox apple
125g (4¼oz/⅔ cup minus 2 tsp) rapadura or light muscovado (soft brown) sugar
30g (1oz/2 tbsp) rapeseed (canola) oil
1 large egg
pinch of sea salt
finely grated zest 1 orange

Preheat the oven to 200°C/fan 180°C/400°F and line a muffin tin with 9 paper cases. If using, toast the walnuts on a baking sheet for 5–6 minutes until lightly browned. Cool, then roughly chop.

Mix together the almond milk and vinegar and allow to sour for 5 minutes.

In a separate bowl, sift together the flours, spices and raising agents.

Grate the pear coarsely, then weigh out 75g/2¾oz. Roughly chop the apple and weigh out 110g/4oz.

In a large bowl, whisk the rapadura, oil, egg and salt into the soured almond milk. Top with the orange zest, pear, apple and walnuts, if using. Add the sifted flours and gently fold them into the mix. Be careful not to overmix.

Fill the muffin cases evenly and bake for 25 minutes, by which time they should be risen and a deep brown colour. Cool on a wire rack until cold. Store in an airtight container for up to 24 hours.

This makes a great alternative Christmas dessert or a superlative pudding for any winter dinner party. Although the recipe involves three separate elements, each comes together pretty quickly and easily, so it's not too challenging.

Chocolate, Rye & Chestnut Roulade

WF | DF

SERVES 6–8

4 eggs
pinch of sea salt
110g (4oz/½ cup plus 1 tbsp) coconut sugar or dark muscovado (soft brown) sugar
25g (1oz/¼ cup) cocoa powder
20g (¾oz/scant ¼ cup) dark rye flour
rapeseed (canola) oil, for greasing

FOR THE CHESTNUT CREAM

100g (3½oz/¾ cup) chestnuts, cooked and peeled
60g (2¼oz/scant ½ cup) soft pitted dates (ideally Medjool)
1 tsp vanilla extract or paste
125g (4¼oz/scant ½ cup) coconut cream

FOR THE GANACHE

125g (4¼oz/scant ½ cup) coconut cream
200g (7oz) dark chocolate (55% cocoa solids), roughly chopped
1 tsp honey

FOR THE COMPOTE

150g (5fl oz/⅔ cup) orange juice
100g (3½oz/1 heaping cup) fresh or frozen cranberries
200g (7oz/generous 1 cup) golden caster (granulated) sugar

Preheat the oven to 200°C/fan 180°C/400°F. Grease a baking sheet or Swiss (jelly roll) tin, 38 x 26cm (15 x 10½in) with oil and line with baking parchment. Whisk the eggs, salt and coconut sugar for 3–4 minutes until light and fluffy. In a separate bowl, sift together the cocoa powder and flour. Fold this into the egg mixture gently until smooth.

Scrape the mixture into the tin and spread out evenly. Bake for 12 minutes, or until starting to brown and shrinking from the sides. Cool completely in the tin on a wire rack.

For the chestnut cream, process the chestnuts in a blender until fine. Add the dates and process until as fine as possible. Add the vanilla and coconut cream, and process again until smooth and creamy. Chill until needed.

For the ganache, place all the ingredients in a heatproof bowl set over a pan of simmering water and melt for 5 minutes, stirring occasionally. Remove and cool slightly, then stir until smooth. Cover the top directly

with clingfilm (plastic wrap) and leave at room temperature for 1 hour to thicken.

To assemble, place the sponge upside down on top of a piece of baking parchment, with a short side closest to you, and peel off the backing paper. Spread with a thin layer of the chestnut cream, leaving a border of 2.5cm (1in) at the top. Use the baking parchment underneath the sponge to help lift and roll it tightly from the bottom. Chill the roulade wrapped in the paper for 20 minutes until firm.

For the compote, heat the orange juice with the cranberries until simmering. Pour in the sugar and stir over a low heat until dissolved. Bring back to the boil and boil steadily for 3–5 minutes. The compote is ready when thickened and holds its shape when placed on a chilled saucer.

Place the roulade on a serving plate. Spread the ganache over the top and sides and chill again until firm. Trim the ends off at an angle, and serve with the compote.

By itself, swede (rutabaga) can be a little overpowering in cakes; quite peppery and distinctive. As a complement to ginger, however, it works well and lends just the right amount of kick and moisture.

Swede & Ginger Cake

DF | VG

MAKES 4 SMALL LOAF CAKES

or a 450-g (1-lb) loaf cake
to serve 4–6

2 tsp ground flaxseed
¼ swede (rutabaga)
1 tsp cider vinegar
60g (2fl oz/¼ cup) unsweetened almond milk
120g (4¼oz/⅔ cup) rapadura sugar or light muscovado (soft brown) sugar
5-cm (2-in) piece of fresh root ginger, peeled and grated
pinch of sea salt
15g (½fl oz/1 tbsp) rapeseed (canola) oil, plus extra for greasing
90g (3¼oz/⅔ cup) khorasan (Kamut®) flour
½ tsp bicarbonate of soda (baking soda)
¼ tsp ground ginger
brown rice syrup or maple syrup, to glaze
crystallized (candied) ginger, to decorate

Preheat the oven to 180°C/fan 160°C/350°F. Grease 4 individual loaf tins or a 450-g (1-lb) loaf tin with rapeseed (canola) oil and line with baking parchment.

Mix the flaxseed with 6 teaspoons of warm water and allow to thicken for 10 minutes.

Meanwhile, peel and grate the swede (rutabaga) coarsely, then weigh out 80g (3oz).

Mix the ground flaxseed with the vinegar, almond milk, rapadura, ginger, salt and oil in a bowl and blend well with a balloon whisk. Fold in the grated swede.

In a separate bowl, sift together the flour, bicarbonate of soda (baking soda) and ginger. Add to the wet ingredients and fold through with a silicone spatula.

Divide the mixture evenly between the tins and bake for 35 minutes for the small tins or 45 minutes for the large one. The top should spring back when pressed and an inserted cocktail stick will come out clean.

Cool in the tin(s) until just warm before de-moulding onto a wire rack to cool completely. When cold, glaze with a little rice syrup or maple syrup, and top with a few pieces of crystallized (candied) ginger.

Basic Recipes

Pastry

MAKES ENOUGH FOR 5 TARTS

or pies 10cm (4in) across or one
20-cm (8-in) tart or pie

2 tsp gram (chickpea) flour
2 tsp ground flaxseed
70g (2½oz/¼ cup) coconut cream
45g (1½oz/¼ cup) coconut oil,
    melted
1 tsp cider vinegar
100g (3½oz/1 cup) oats (gluten
    free if needed)
40g (1½oz/⅓ cup) rice flour
60g (2¼oz/⅔ cup) ground almonds
60g (2¼oz/5 tbsp) rapadura or
    light soft brown sugar
large pinch of salt
¼ tsp xanthan gum (optional)

WF | GF | DF | VG

Mix together the gram flour, flaxseed, coconut cream, coconut oil and vinegar with a small whisk until well blended. Chill for 30 minutes, or until cool and firmed.

Process the oats in a blender until fine. Add the rice flour, ground almonds, rapadura, salt and xanthan gum, if using, processing again to mix.

Pour the dry ingredients into a bowl, add the chilled wet ingredients and blend together using a spatula or your fingertips. Knead gently to form a smooth, soft dough. Flatten, wrap in clingfilm (plastic wrap) and chill for at least 1 hour, or up to 3 days.

For individual tarts and pies, divide the dough into equal pieces before rolling out between 2 sheets of baking parchment until 3mm (⅛in) thick. For one large tart or pie, roll all the dough out between 2 sheets of baking parchment to 4mm (⅙in) thick. Use to line the tart tins by lifting off the top piece of baking parchment, flipping the pastry over and gently resting on top of the tin. Peel off the paper, then tuck the edges of the pastry into the corners of the tin. Gently knock off the excess pastry, then press the pastry into the bottom and sides. Chill for 30 minutes before baking as directed in the recipe.

Cheesecake Base

MAKES ENOUGH FOR 8 SMALL CAKES
or one 15-cm (6-in) cake

45g (1½oz/⅓ cup) whole almonds, unskinned
15g (½fl oz/1 tbsp) coconut oil
10g (¼oz/2 tsp) cashew nut butter
10g (¼oz/2 tsp) maple syrup
55g (2oz/½ cup) oats (gluten-free if needed)
30g (1oz/2½ tbsp) coconut sugar or dark muscovado (soft brown) sugar
½ tsp ground cinnamon
pinch of sea salt
5g (⅛oz/1 tsp) desiccated (dry unsweetened) coconut

WF | GF | DF | VG

Preheat the oven to 200°C/fan 180°C/400°F. Toast the almonds on a baking sheet for 5–6 minutes until just browned. Cool. Reduce the oven temperature to 180°C/fan 160°C/350°F.

Melt the coconut oil, then add the cashew nut butter and maple syrup and whisk together to blend well.

Finely grind the almonds with the oats in a blender, then add the coconut sugar, cinnamon and salt, and blend again. Add the wet mixture and blend again until the mix comes together. Mix in the desiccated (dry unsweetened) coconut by hand. Divide the mixture equally between your chosen silicone moulds or into a lined tin and press down. Place on a baking sheet and bake for 15 minutes, or until browned around the edges. Cool on a wire rack.

Vegan Pastry Cream

MAKES ENOUGH FOR 5 SMALL TARTS
or one 20-cm (8-in) tart or pie

200g (7fl oz/scant 1 cup) unsweetened almond milk
200g (7oz/¾ cup) coconut cream, chilled
2 strips of zest from 1 unwaxed lemon
1 vanilla pod (bean), split in half lengthways and seeds scraped out
30g (1oz/¼ cup) cornflour (cornstarch)
60g (2¼oz/⅓ cup) golden caster (granulated) sugar or demerara (raw brown) sugar
30g (1oz/2 tbsp) cashew nut butter

WF | GF | DF | VG

Place the almond milk and 50g (1¾oz/¼ cup) of the coconut cream in a small pan with the lemon zest and vanilla pod (bean). Heat to almost boiling, then turn off the heat, cover and infuse for 30 minutes.

Mix together the cornflour (cornstarch), sugar and vanilla seeds in a bowl. Remove the vanilla pod and lemon zest from the cooled, infused liquid mix and use 1 tablespoon of this to blend with the cornflour and sugar. Stir until smooth.

Return the milk mixture to the pan and heat over a medium-high heat until it just comes to the boil. Gradually pour half of the hot liquid over the sugar-cornflour mix, stirring with a whisk, then pour this into the pan and cook over a medium-high heat, stirring constantly. It should be gently bubbling. Cook for 4–5 minutes, or until thick. Mix in the cashew nut butter, then scrape into a bowl. Cover the surface directly with clingfilm (plastic wrap) and cool to room temperature. Chill until completely cold.

Whip the remaining coconut cream for 2 minutes with a whisk until it has loosened and forms soft peaks. Use the whisk to beat the cold nut butter and milk mixture for 1 minute until smooth. Add the coconut cream to this and beat until it is evenly incorporated, smooth, light and creamy. Use to fill the tart cases, or chill for up to 3 days before use.

Custard

MAKES APPROX 350G (13OZ)

4 egg yolks
45g (1½oz/3¼ tbsp) golden caster
  (granulated) sugar or demerara
  (raw brown) sugar
2 tbsp cornflour (cornstarch)
1 vanilla pod (bean), split in
  half lengthways and seeds
  scraped out
150g (5¼oz/⅔ cup) coconut cream
125g (4fl oz/½ cup) unsweetened
  almond milk

WF | GF | DF

Mix together the egg yolks,
sugar and cornflour (cornstarch)
in a heatproof bowl. Add the
vanilla seeds and place the empty
pod in a small pan. Add the
coconut cream and almond milk
to the pan, and bring gently to
the boil, stirring occasionally.
As soon as it comes to the boil,
gradually pour over the egg
yolk mix, stirring constantly.
Pour the mixture back into the
pan and cook gently for 5–6
minutes, stirring constantly.
If the mixture starts to become
lumpy, remove from the heat
and stir with a balloon whisk to
blend the custard back together.
When ready, the custard will
be thick, smooth and not taste
'floury'. Cool for a few minutes
before using.

Vegan Custard

MAKES APPROX 500G (1LB 2OZ)

150g (5¼fl oz/⅔ cup) unsweetened
  almond milk
250g (8¾oz/generous ¾ cup)
  coconut cream
2 strips of pared zest from
  1 unwaxed lemon
1 vanilla pod (bean), split in
  half lengthways and seeds
  scraped out
15g (½oz/2 tbsp) cornflour
  (cornstarch)
60g (2¼oz/⅓ cup) golden caster
  (granulated) sugar or demerara
  (raw brown) sugar
30g (1oz/2 tbsp) cashew nut butter

WF | GF | DF | VG

Place the almond milk and
coconut cream in a small pan.
Add the pared lemon strips and
empty vanilla pod (bean) and
heat to almost boiling point.
Turn off the heat, cover and
infuse for 30 minutes.

Mix together the cornflour
(cornstarch), sugar and vanilla
seeds in a heatproof bowl.
Remove the vanilla pod and
lemon zest from the liquid mix
and use 1 tablespoon of the
cooled mix to blend with the
cornflour and sugar. Stir until
smooth.

Return the milk and cream
mixture to a medium-high heat
and heat until it just comes to
the boil, then gradually pour
half of this hot liquid over the
sugar-cornflour mix, stirring.

Pour this mixture back into the
pan and cook, stirring, over
a medium-high heat for 4–5
minutes, or until thickened,
smooth and has lost its 'floury'
taste. Mix in the cashew nut
butter. Serve or transfer to a
heatproof jug and cover directly
with clingfilm (plastic wrap).
Reheat before serving.

Candied Orange or Lemon Strips

2 unwaxed oranges or lemons
100g (3½oz/½ cup) golden caster
  (granulated) sugar

Use a julienne peeler to peel off long thin strips from the zest of the oranges or lemons. Place in a small pan, cover with cold water and bring to the boil. Drain and repeat this blanching process twice more, straining each time.

Place the orange or lemon strips in the pan with the sugar and 100g (3½oz/7 tbsp) water and bring gently to the boil, stirring to dissolve the sugar. Boil for 1 minute, then remove from the heat and let the strips steep in the warm syrup until cold. Chill the strips in the syrup in an airtight container for up to 2 weeks.

Candied Orange Slices

225g (8oz/1¼ cups) golden caster
  (granulated) sugar
1 unwaxed orange, halved and cut
  into roughly 3–4mm (⅛–⅙in)
  thick slices

Place the sugar and 150g (5oz/⅔ cup) water into a small pan and heat to dissolve the sugar and bring the syrup just to the boil.

When the syrup reaches the boil, add the orange slices and cover them with foil or baking parchment to keep them submerged in the syrup. Simmer very gently for 45 minutes, or until the orange slices are translucent. Remove from the heat and allow the fruit to cool in the pan.

Transfer to an airtight container and chill for at least 24 hours before using (so the orange slices can absorb the syrup). The candied orange slices will keep for up to 4 weeks in the fridge. Drain and slice into quarters before using.

Candied Carrot Strips

200g (7oz/1 cup) golden caster (granulated) sugar
1 small carrot

Dissolve the sugar in 100g (3½fl oz/7 tbsp) water in a small pan and bring to a gentle simmer. Remove from the heat.

Peel the carrot. Use a vegetable peeler to pare off thin strips from the vegetable, peeling both sides until you have removed as much as you can. Place the strips directly into the hot syrup and cook gently, covered, for 2–3 minutes until the vegetable is just tender and translucent.

Remove from the heat and steep in the syrup overnight at room temperature. For different coloured carrots, start by candying a few yellow strips, then remove from the pan and let them steep in a little of the syrup. Reuse the remaining syrup to candy the orange strips, and finally the purple strips.

Store the candied strips in the syrup in the fridge for up to a week and drain from the syrup before topping the cakes.

Candied Blood Orange Crisps

1 blood orange
150g (5¼oz/¾ cup) golden caster (granulated) sugar

Slice the orange in half lengthways, and using a sharp serrated knife, cut very thin slices (less than 1mm/¹⁄₁₆in) from both pieces. Discard any pips. Place the orange slices gently onto the bottom of a wide pan.

In a separate small pan, mix together the sugar and 150g (5oz/⅔ cup) water and bring the mixture to the boil. Boil for 1 minute, then remove from the heat and pour over the orange slices. Cover the pan with a lid and allow the slices to steep in a warm place overnight.

The next day, uncover and warm the pan over a medium-low heat until the sugar syrup begins to steam, but does not boil. Replace the lid and leave overnight again.

The next day, gently remove the slices using a small palette knife and place onto a baking sheet lined with baking parchment. Preheat the oven to 100°C/fan 80°C/210°F and place the baking sheet in the centre of the oven. Prop the oven door open slightly using a wooden spoon, so the moist air can escape and dry the orange slices, for 1½ hours, keeping an eye on them to make sure they don't brown. If you notice any coloration, reduce the temperature. Once they are dry enough to gently lift off the paper, turn them over and put them back in the oven for another 30 minutes.

Cool on a wire rack. Store in an airtight container in between layers of baking parchment.

Candied Kumquats

150g (5¼oz) kumquats
150g (5¼oz/¾ cup) golden caster
    (granulated) sugar

Slice the kumquats into 3–4mm
(⅛–⅙in) thick rounds, or
halve lengthways and discard
the seeds.

Dissolve the sugar in 100g
(3½oz/7 tbsp) water in a small
pan. Bring to a gentle simmer
and add the kumquats. Cover
them directly with a piece of
foil or baking parchment to
keep them submerged in the
syrup. Cook, covered, over a low
heat for 15 minutes, or until
translucent and tender.

Remove from the heat and cool,
uncovered. Transfer to a covered
container and chill for up to
2 weeks.

Candied Rhubarb Twists

200g (7oz/1 cup) golden caster
    (granulated) sugar
1 rhubarb stalk

Dissolve the sugar in 150g
(5floz/⅔ cup) water in a pan
and bring to a gentle simmer.
Remove from the heat.

Use a vegetable peeler to pare
off 1mm (⅓₂in) thick strips
of the rhubarb, keeping them
the whole length of the stalk if
possible. Place the strips into the
pan of syrup, making sure they
are all covered, and leave for
30 minutes.

Preheat the oven to 100°C/fan
80°C/210°F and line a baking
sheet with non-stick baking
parchment. Drain the rhubarb
from the syrup and lay the slices
out flat on the paper. Place in
the oven for 45–60 minutes until
the slices have dried out but still
with a little flexibility.

Grease the handles of some
wooden spoons with a little
coconut oil. Working with 1 slice
of rhubarb at a time, quickly
wind it around the handle to
form a spiral. It should just be
flexible enough to do this while
warm, but then firm up and set
as it cools. If it is too flexible and
doesn't hold its shape, return
the rhubarb to the oven for
5–10 minutes. Once the rhubarb
spirals have cooled and set,
remove from the support and
keep in an airtight container in a
cool dry place until needed.

Candied Beetroot Slices or Hearts

2 small beetroots
120g (4¼oz/⅔ cup minus 2 tsp)
    unrefined (golden) cane sugar

Use a sharp knife to cut very
thin rounds, about 1mm (⅓₂in)
horizontally through the
beetroots.

Heat together the sugar and 75g
(2½oz/5 tbsp) water in a small
pan until the sugar is dissolved
and the mixture comes to the
boil. Place the beetroot directly
into the hot syrup, cover and
cook gently for 5 minutes until
the beetroot is just tender and
translucent.

Remove from the heat and steep
in the syrup overnight at room
temperature. Chill the candied
slices in the syrup for up to a
week and drain from the syrup
before decorating the cakes.

For heart shapes, use a small
heart cutter to cut shapes from
the centre of the beetroot rounds.

For crisp beetroot hearts, used
on the top of the Beetroot Red
Velvet Cake (pages 94–6), drain
the pieces from the syrup and
lay on top of baking parchment
over a wire rack. Dry for 1½
hours in a low oven (100°C/fan
80°C/210°F), turning halfway,
until dried through.

Ingredient Index

Ingredients are everything when it comes to free-from baking. I have worked hard to ensure all the ingredients I've sourced are natural, healthy, varied and pretty easy to find in local shops. My primary objective is to encourage and inspire bakers to explore a wider range of ingredients than usual, whether in the form of unrefined (golden) sugars or various types of wheat-free/heirloom flours. Here you will find a list of ingredients, their benefits to the bake and their full description to help to inform and eventually empower you to continue on your own free-from kitchen journey of exploration.

FLOURS & DRY INGREDIENTS

My recipes utilise a wide variety of flours in varying proportions versus a single flour-blend used for every recipe. This approach allows you to experience the tastes and textures unique to each.

WHOLEMEAL (WHOLEWHEAT) RYE:

One of my favourite flours, rye is used in German and Scandanavian baking to produce hearty nutritious breads, but it also works well in sweet baking. Rye flour is suitable for those with a wheat intolerance and provides more fibre, so is better at controlling blood sugar levels.

WHOLEMEAL SPELT:

An ancient relative to wheat, spelt contains gluten but has a slightly different nutritional profile to conventional wheat. It is higher in soluble fibre, so better for digestion and lowering blood sugar levels.

KHORASAN (KAMUT®) FLOUR:

Another ancient variety of wheat, this flour has a distinctive yellow colour and slightly buttery flavour. It has been shown to provoke fewer irritable bowel syndrome (IBS) symptoms and reduce inflammation compared to conventional wheat flour.

RICE FLOUR:

White rice flour has a neutral flavour and is good as a bulking agent in gluten-free recipes. It contains few nutrients, so is best used in conjunction with higher-fibre or more nutritious flours. Brown rice flour is more nutritious and heartier as the fibre, antioxidants, vitamins and minerals have not been stripped out in the refinement process.

BUCKWHEAT FLOUR:

A great whole grain with a distinctive, almost bitter flavour, it pairs well with chocolate and citrus flavours. Buckwheat is rich in antioxidants, particularly rutin, which helps reduce inflammation, cholesterol levels and the risk of cardiovascular disease.

WHITE TEFF FLOUR:

This is a nutrient-dense ancient grain and is an excellent source of amino acids and fibre. It is good used in cakes or pancakes, as it has a less prominent flavour than buckwheat.

OAT FLOUR:

Make your own by processing rolled oats until fine, or buy it already ready ground. If baking for the gluten-intolerant, buy gluten-free oats, as they are frequently processed in facilities that also process wheat, so there can be cross-contamination issues. Oats and oat flour are a great source of soluble fibre, helping to support gut health, reduce bad cholesterol levels and also help with weight loss.

TAPIOCA/CORNFLOUR (CORNSTARCH):

These starchy flours are high in carbohydrates and contain few nutrients. They are helpful in baking to provide structure and a lighter texture than whole grain flours alone. These flours have been used sparingly throughout.

SUGARS

Nutritionally, there is not a huge difference between different sugars, but choosing less refined versions and sticking with natural, rather than artificial, sweeteners will be better for your health and the environment.

RAPADURA SUGAR:

This is an unrefined form of cane sugar, with a distinctive caramel flavour. If you can't find it, use coconut sugar or light muscovado (soft brown) sugar instead. Nutritionally, it is similar to table sugar but goes through less refining so has a lower environmental impact and retains more of the molasses flavour.

COCONUT SUGAR:

Made from the sap of flower buds from the coconut palm tree, this sugar has a deep caramel-molasses flavour that works well in chocolate or stronger flavoured bakes. It contains some minerals and other nutrients, as well as inulin, which may slow glucose absorption and help keep blood sugar levels more balanced compared to table sugar.

MAPLE SYRUP:

This is derived from the sap of maple trees, and has a higher concentration of minerals than table sugar, especially zinc and manganese. It has a slightly lower glycaemic index, so will be slower to raise blood sugar levels.

HONEY: Try to buy local honey where possible; the less intensively farmed the honey, the better quality and more nutritious the product. Raw honey (non-heat treated) naturally contains more nutrients.

DATE SYRUP: Probably the most nutritionally rich of the various sugar options; date syrup has a similar flavour to black treacle (blackstrap molasses), but contains more vitamins, minerals and antioxidants, and has proven antibacterial effects. It works well in any recipe you might use molasses, as it has quite a strong and dark flavour.

BROWN RICE SYRUP: This is a useful honey substitute for vegans, as it has a similar viscosity and mild flavour, but use sparingly as the high glucose content can send blood sugars soaring.

FATS/DAIRY ALTERNATIVES

RAPESEED (CANOLA) OIL: This healthy sustainably grown oil is the best all-round choice as it can be subjected to high baking temperatures without destroying the nutritional value or producing harmful compounds. The delicate flavour means that it works well in a variety of recipes, without interfering with other flavours.

COCONUT OIL: This oil works well in baking as it resists high temperatures without destroying its nutritional value. It also adds creaminess to cheesecakes, as it is solid at room temperature. Although high in saturated fats, these are metabolized differently and may help balance out cholesterol levels. Use good-quality organic and ethically sourced coconut oil.

COCONUT CREAM: This is a helpful dairy substitute. Use either the cream that separates from a can of coconut milk or buy coconut cream already separated. It is lighter in fat than whipping cream so needs

delicate handling to not overwork it. Keep it well chilled as it is less stable. Try to buy organic.

EGGS: Sourcing of quality organic eggs is important for many reasons. Not only are eggs high in nutrients and a great source of protein, but careful selection also helps ensure a higher standard of animal welfare sustainability.

BUTTER: I prefer to use either good-quality unsalted butter or a dairy alternative such as nut butter, coconut oil or a blend of ingredients such as rapeseed oil and vegetable purees. I have, however, excluded the use of dairy butter in this book, in keeping with the free-from nature of all the recipes. I avoid using margarine, since it is much higher in artificial ingredients, and tends to contain harmful fats.

NUTS: Ground nuts help add extra richness and moisture to baked goods. Whole or chopped nuts also add extra texture and flavour, as well as nutrients, while soaking nuts helps to give them a creamier texture for the cheesecakes. Nuts and nut butters bring a variety of extra nutrients and protein to the recipes; most notably, pecans have been shown to help reduce cholesterol level, almonds help boost gut health and cashews are a great source of magnesium for bone and heart health.

FRUIT & VEGETABLES: Including these in your baking is a fantastic way of getting extra fibre and other nutrients. As a large proportion of the nutrients are stored just under the skin of fruit and vegetables, washing or scrubbing is preferable to peeling. Microwaving, baking whole or steaming are the best ways of cooking vegetables to retain their nutrients if you are adding them in a puréed form. Berries are high in antioxidants and good for the heart; apples help reduce cholesterol; citrus fruit, squash and sweet potatoes help boost immunity; swede (rutabaga)

is a great source of minerals, beetroot boosts stamina and carrots are rich in beta-carotene, which is beneficial for eye health.

OTHER INGREDIENTS

SPICES: These are helpful in adding depth of flavour to cakes, curbing the need for more sugar, as well as extra nutrients and antioxidants. Cinnamon, turmeric and ginger are great anti-inflammatories.

COCOA/CACAO POWDER: A natural stimulant and mood booster. You can use standard cocoa powder, although raw cacao generally has a higher nutritional content, having been roasted at lower temperatures.

DARK CHOCOLATE: I use two types of chocolate in the book – 70% and 55%, which are both dairy-free. The higher the cocoa percentage, the greater the health benefits. For ganaches or recipes that require a gentler flavour, I use a lower percentage dark chocolate.

SEA SALT: Necessary for boosting flavour, my go-to sea salt is Maldon, since it has a great flavour and soft flakes. I occasionally use Himalayan pink sea salt.

PSYLLIUM HUSK/XANTHAN GUM: Both of these mimic the action of gluten in baked goods, helping to hold batters and sponges together. Generally, psyllium husk is a more natural ingredient and less likely to cause any digestive issues for people with sensitive guts. It works well in batters and sponges, but for drier bakes such as pastry, xanthan gum is more effective at binding.

Index

A

almond (ground)
  banana buckwheat pancakes 48–9
  beetroot red velvet cake 95–6
  buckwheat, citrus & lavender
    sablés 31
  caramel & chocolate mini cakes 70
  carrot, orange & pistachio cakes
    50
  chocolate aubergine fondant 108
  chocolate beetroot domes 77–9
  Christmas fruit & root cake with
    candied fruit & glazed nuts
    121–3
  courgette, gooseberry &
    elderflower layer cake 45–7
  lemon & Earl Grey loaf cakes 22
  lime, coconut & courgette cake 14
  marquise au chocolat 86
  orange, butternut & poppy seed
    loaf 28
  passion fruit & parsnip mini cakes
    34
  pastry 25, 64, 130
  peach, rosemary & olive oil
    friands 59
  rhubarb & orange bundt cakes 20
  spiced blood orange & clementine
    cake 112
  spicy vegan chocolate cake 119–20
  sticky toffee pudding with toffee
    sauce 97–8
  summer berry layer cake with
    coconut cream 42
almond (whole, unskinned) 131
almond butter 116
almond milk 132
apple 121–3, 124
apricot (dried) 121–3
aubergine chocolate fondant 108–9
avocado & olive oil chocolate
  mousse 56–7

B

baking basics 8–9
balsamic reductions 53
banana
  banana buckwheat pancakes 48–9
  banana walnut loaf 82–3
basil
  lemon & basil posset 26–7
  strawberry & basil tart 52–3
beetroot
  beetroot red velvet cake 94–6
  candied beetroot slices or hearts

94–6, 135
  chocolate beetroot domes 77–9
berries
  summer berry layer cake with
    coconut cream 42–4
  see also specific berries
biscuits
  buckwheat, citrus & lavender
    sablés 30–1
  buckwheat, hazelnut & cinnamon
    shorties 80–1
  see also cookies; shortbread
blood orange
  candied blood orange crisps 134
  spiced blood orange & clementine
    cake 112–13
blood sugar levels 6
blueberry & lime cheesecakes
  12–13
bread, quick date & pecan 90–1
brown rice flour 34, 50, 59, 86,
  119–20, 131–3
brown rice syrup 12, 40, 62, 104,
  115, 128, 137
brown teff flour 90
brownies, pecan-studded sweet
  potato 68–9
buckwheat flour 136
  banana buckwheat pancakes 48–9
  beetroot red velvet cake 95–6
  buckwheat, hazelnut & cinnamon
    shorties 81
  caramel & chocolate mini cakes 70
  carrot, orange & pistachio cakes
    50
  chocolate beetroot domes 77–9
  Christmas fruit & root cake with
    candied fruit & glazed nuts
    121–3
  citrus & lavender sablés 30–1
  hazelnut & cinnamon shorties
    80–1
  pastry 25, 64
  rye, buckwheat & winter fruit
    muffins 124–5
  spiced caramel bundt cake 106
  sticky toffee pudding with toffee
    sauce 97–8
bundt cakes
  pumpkin, khorasan & chai 100–1
  rhubarb & orange 20–1
  spiced caramel 106–7
butter 137
butternut squash
  caramel & chocolate mini cakes 70

orange, butternut & poppy seed
    loaf 28–9
  spiced pumpkin pies 93
  summer berry layer cake with
    coconut cream 42

C

cakes
  banana walnut loaf 82–3
  beetroot red velvet cake 94–6
  caramel & chocolate mini cakes
    70–2
  carrot, orange & pistachio cakes
    50–1
  Christmas fruit & root cake with
    candied fruit & glazed nuts
    121–3
  courgette (zucchini), gooseberry &
    elderflower layer cake 45–7
  heritage carrot layer cake 73–6
  lemon & Earl Grey loaf cakes 22–3
  orange, butternut & poppy seed
    loaf 28–9
  passion fruit & parsnip mini cakes
    34–5
  pumpkin, khorasan & chai bundt
    cakes 100–1
  rhubarb & orange bundt cakes
    20–1
  rye, buckwheat & winter fruit
    muffins 124–5
  spiced blood orange & clementine
    cake 112–13
  spiced caramel bundt cake 106–7
  spicy vegan chocolate cake 118–20
  summer berry layer cake with
    coconut cream 42–4
  swede & ginger cake 128–9
candied beetroot slices or hearts
  95–6, 135
candied blood orange crisps 134
candied carrot strips 73–6, 134
candied kumquats 121–3, 135
candied orange slices 28–9, 54, 133
candied orange strips 25, 104, 133
candied rhubarb twists 135
caramel
  caramel & chocolate mini cakes
    70–2
  salted caramel & chocolate tarts
    114–15
  salted caramel filling 70–2, 84
  spiced caramel bundt cake 106–7
carrot
  candied carrot strips 134

Christmas fruit & root cake with candied fruit & glazed nuts 121–3
heritage carrot layer cake 73–6
orange & pistachio cakes 50–1
cashew nut
chai & cashew shortbread 12, 32, 40–1, 110–11
cheesecakes 12, 88
spiced pumpkin pies 93
cashew nut butter
chai & cashew shortbread 110–11
cheesecake base recipe 131
hipster shortbread 84
rye cocoa-nut cookies 116
salted caramel & chocolate tarts 115
salted caramel filling 72, 84
spicy vegan chocolate cake 119–20
vegan custard 132
vegan pastry cream 131
chai spice mix
chai & cashew shortbread 110–11
chai latte cheesecakes 88–9
pumpkin, khorasan & chai bundt cakes 100–1
recipe 88
spicy vegan chocolate cake 119–20
cheesecakes
blueberry & lime 12–13
chai latte 88–9
cheesecake base recipe 131
mango & passion fruit 40–1
vanilla 32–3
chestnut, chocolate & rye roulade 126–7
chickpea (gram) flour 25, 130
chickpea(s) 17–19
chocolate 137
caramel & chocolate mini cakes 70–2
chocolate aubergine fondant 108–9
chocolate beetroot domes 77–9
chocolate caramel ganache 72
chocolate ganache 79, 126
chocolate ganache filling 86
chocolate ganache with mulled wine spices 112
chocolate ganache topping 115
chocolate ganache toppings 104
chocolate orange tarts with Mayan spices 104–5
coconut chocolate ganache 119–20
ginger-chocolate & orange frozen tart 54–5
marquise au chocolat 86–7
olive oil & avocado chocolate mousse 56–7
pecan-studded sweet potato brownies 68
rye & chestnut roulade 126–7
salted caramel & chocolate tarts 114–15

salted caramel filling for hipster shortbread 84
spicy vegan chocolate cake 118–20
Christmas fruit & root cake with candied fruit & glazed nuts 121–3
cinnamon 48, 70, 73, 82, 88, 90, 93, 104, 106, 112, 123, 124, 131, 137
buckwheat & hazelnut shorties 80–1
clementine & blood orange spiced cake 112–13
cocoa nibs 116
cocoa/cacao powder 70, 77, 95, 108, 119, 126, 137
coconut cream 137
blueberry & lime cheesecakes 12
chai latte cheesecakes 88
chestnut cream 126
chocolate caramel ganache 72
chocolate ganache topping 104, 115
coconut Chantilly cream 26–7, 44
coconut chocolate ganache 119–20
coconut crème fraîche 108
custard 132
elderflower cream 47
fig & honey tarts 64
ganache 126
ganache filling 86
ginger-chocolate & orange frozen tart 54
lemon & basil posset 27
lime curd 14
mango & passion fruit cheesecake 40
olive oil & avocado chocolate mousse 56
pastry 25, 130
pistachio & raspberry tart 62
rhubarb & orange cream 20
rosewater coconut cream 50
simple summer trifle 61
spiced pumpkin pies 93
summer berry layer cake with coconut cream 42–4
vanilla cheesecake 32
vanilla coconut frosting 96
vegan custard 132
vegan pastry cream 131
coconut (desiccated) 84, 116, 131
lime, coconut & courgette cake 14–16
coconut oil 137
coconut sugar 136
compote
cranberry & orange 126
gooseberry 45–7
rhubarb & strawberry 36
cookies, rye cocoa-nut 116–17
cornflour (cornstarch/tapioca flour) 14, 17, 20, 59, 72, 82, 106, 112,

119, 131–2, 136
courgette (zucchini)
gooseberry & elderflower layer cake 45–7
lemon & Earl Grey loaf cakes 22
lime, coconut & courgette (zucchini) cake 14–16
summer berry layer cake with coconut cream 42
cranberry & orange compote 126
creamed coconut 73–6, 96
crème fraîche, coconut 108
curd, lime 14
currant(s) 121–3
custard 61, 132
rhubarb & custard tarts 24–5
vegan custard 97–8, 132

D
dairy alternatives 137
date(s)
chestnut cream 126
date & pecan quick bread 90–1
olive oil & avocado chocolate mousse 56
pecan-studded sweet potato brownies 68
salted caramel filling 70–2, 84, 115
sticky toffee pudding with toffee sauce 97–8
date syrup 97, 98, 137

E
Earl Grey tea 97–8
lemon & Earl Grey loaf cakes 22–3
egg 137
caramel & chocolate mini cakes 70
carrot, orange & pistachio cakes 50
chocolate, rye & chestnut roulade 126–7
chocolate aubergine fondant 108
chocolate beetroot domes 77–9
Christmas fruit & root cake with candied fruit & glazed nuts 121–3
courgette, gooseberry & elderflower layer cake 45–7
custard 132
date & pecan bread 90
heritage carrot layer cake 73–6
lemon & Earl Grey loaf cakes 22
lime, coconut & courgette cake 14
lime curd 14
marquise au chocolat 86
orange, butternut & poppy seed loaf 28
passion fruit & parsnip mini cakes 34
peach, rosemary & olive oil friands 59

pecan-studded sweet potato
 brownies 68
rhubarb, strawberry & parsnip
 roulade 36–7
rhubarb & orange bundt cakes 20
rye, buckwheat & winter fruit
 muffins 124
spiced blood orange & clementine
 cake 112
spiced caramel bundt cake 106
summer berry layer cake with
 coconut cream 42
elderflower
courgette, gooseberry &
 elderflower layer cake 45–7
elderflower cream 47
equipment 9

F
fats 137
fig & honey tarts 64–5
flaxseed (ground)
beetroot red velvet cake 95–6
buckwheat, citrus & lavender
 sablés 31
buckwheat, hazelnut & cinnamon
 shorties 81
Christmas fruit & root cake with
 candied fruit & glazed nuts
 121–3
courgette (zucchini), gooseberry &
 elderflower layer cake 45–7
date & pecan bread 90
lime, coconut & courgette
 (zucchini) cake 14–16
pastry 25, 64, 130
pumpkin, khorasan & chai bundt
 cakes 100
rhubarb & custard tarts 24–5
spicy vegan chocolate cake 119–20
sticky toffee pudding with toffee
 sauce 97–8
summer berry layer cake with
 coconut cream 42
swede & ginger cake 128
flours 8–9, 136
see also specific flours
fondant, chocolate aubergine 108–9
friands, peach, rosemary & olive
 oil 58–9
frosting
lemon coconut 73–6
vanilla coconut 96
see also icing
fruit 137
see also specific fruit
fruit cake, Christmas fruit & root
 cake with candied fruit & glazed
 nuts 121–3

G
ganache 126
chocolate caramel ganache 72
chocolate ganache 79
chocolate ganache with mulled
 wine spices 112
chocolate ganache topping 104,
 115
coconut chocolate ganache 119–20
ganache filling 86
ginger
ginger-chocolate & orange frozen
 tart 54–5
swede & ginger cake 128–9
glacé icing 28–9, 106
glaze, passion fruit 34
gluten 8
gluten-free baking basics 8–9
gluten-free flours 8–9, 136
goji berry 121–3
gooseberry, elderflower & courgette
 layer cake 45–7
gram (chickpea) flour 25, 130

H
hazelnut 100
hazelnut, buckwheat, & cinnamon
 shorties 80–1
honey 79, 108, 112, 137
fig & honey tarts 64–5

I
icing
Earl Grey 22–3
glacé 28–9, 106
see also frosting

K
khorasan (Kamut®) flour 100–1,
 110, 128, 136
kumquat, candied 121–3, 135

L
lavender, buckwheat & citrus
 sablés 30–1
layer cakes 14–16, 42–7, 73–6,
 94–6, 118–20
lemon
buckwheat, citrus & lavender
 sablés 31
candied lemon strips 133
lemon & basil posset 26–7
lemon & Earl Grey loaf cakes
 22–3, 61
lemon coconut frosting 73–6
lemon meringue pies 17–19
lime
blueberry & lime cheesecakes
 12–13
lime curd 14
loaf cakes
banana walnut 82–3

lemon & Earl Grey 22–3
orange, butternut & poppy seed
 28–9

M
mango & passion fruit cheesecake
 40–1
maple syrup 136
marquise au chocolat 86–7
measurements 8
meringue
lemon meringue pies 17–19
vegan meringue 17–19
'mis-en-place' 8
mousse, olive oil & avocado
 chocolate 56–7
muffins, rye, buckwheat & winter
 fruit 124–5
mulled wine spices & chocolate
 ganache 112

N
nuts 137
see also specific nuts

O
oat(s) 28, 130, 131
oat flour 28, 136
olive oil
olive oil & avocado chocolate
 mousse 56–7
peach, rosemary & olive oil
 friands 58–9
orange
buckwheat, citrus & lavender
 sablés 31
candied blood orange crisps 134
candied orange slices 133
candied orange strips 133
carrot, orange & pistachio cakes
 50–1
chocolate orange tarts with Mayan
 spices 104–5
cranberry & orange compote 126
ginger-chocolate & orange frozen
 tart 54–5
orange, butternut & poppy seed
 loaf 28–9
rhubarb & orange bundt cakes
 20–1
spiced blood orange & clementine
 cake 112–13
organization 8
ovens 8

P
pancakes, banana buckwheat 48–9
parsnip
passion fruit & parsnip mini cakes
 34–5
rhubarb, strawberry & parsnip
 roulade 36–7

passion fruit
  mango & passion fruit cheesecake 40–1
  passion fruit & parsnip mini cakes 34–5
pastry cream, vegan 24–5, 53, 131
pastry dishes
  chocolate orange tarts with Mayan spices 104–5
  fig & honey tarts 64–5
  lemon meringue pies 17–19
  pastry recipes 25, 64, 130
  pistachio & raspberry tart 62–3
  rhubarb & custard tarts 24–5
  salted caramel & chocolate tarts 114–15
  spiced pumpkin pies 92–3
  strawberry & basil tart 52–3
peach, rosemary & olive oil friands 58–9
pear 124
pecan 84, 97–8
  date & pecan bread 90–1
  pecan-studded sweet potato brownies 68–9
pies
  lemon meringue 17–19
  spiced pumpkin 92–3
pistachio 61, 86
  carrot, orange & pistachio cakes 50–1
  pistachio & raspberry tart 62–3
poppy seed, orange & butternut loaf 28–9
posset, lemon & basil 26–7
psyllium husk 8, 34, 70, 77, 137
pumpkin
  khorasan & chai bundt cakes 100–1
  spiced pumpkin pies 92–3

R
raisin(s) 121–3
rapadura sugar 136
rapeseed (canola) oil 137
raspberry 61
  pistachio & raspberry tart 62–3
red velvet cake, beetroot 94–6
rhubarb
  candied rhubarb twists 135
  rhubarb, strawberry & parsnip roulade 36–7
  rhubarb & custard tarts 24–5
  rhubarb & orange bundt cakes 20–1
rice flour 136
  buckwheat, citrus & lavender sablés 31
  courgette, gooseberry & elderflower layer cake 45–7
  date & pecan bread 90
  lemon & Earl Grey loaf cakes 22

lime, coconut & courgette cake 14
orange, butternut & poppy seed loaf 28
pastry 25, 64, 130
rhubarb, strawberry & parsnip roulade 36
rhubarb & orange bundt cakes 20
spiced blood orange & clementine cake 112
spiced caramel bundt cake 106
sticky toffee pudding with toffee sauce 97–8
summer berry layer cake with coconut cream 42
see also brown rice flour
rosewater coconut cream 50
roulades
  chocolate, rye & chestnut 126–7
  rhubarb, strawberry & parsnip 36–7
rutabaga see swede
rye
  chocolate, rye & chestnut roulade 126–7
  rye, buckwheat & winter fruit muffins 124–5
  rye cocoa-nut cookies 116–17
  see also wholemeal rye flour

S
sablés, buckwheat, citrus & lavender 30–1
salt 137
salted caramel
  salted caramel & chocolate tarts 114–15
  salted caramel filling 70–2, 84
shortbread
  chai & cashew 110–11
  hipster 84–5
shorties, buckwheat, hazelnut & cinnamon 80–1
soya milk (wholebean) 90
spelt flour (wholemeal) 95–6
spices 137
  chocolate ganache with mulled wine spices 112
  chocolate orange tarts with Mayan spices 104–5
  spiced blood orange & clementine cake 112–13
  spiced caramel bundt cake 106–7
  spiced pumpkin pies 92–3
  spicy vegan chocolate cake 118–20
  see also specific spices
sticky toffee pudding with toffee sauce 97–9
strawberry
  rhubarb, strawberry & parsnip roulade 36–7
  strawberry & basil tart 52–3
sugars 136–7

sultana(s) 121–3
summer berry layer cake with coconut cream 42–4
swede
  Christmas fruit & root cake with candied fruit & glazed nuts 121–3
  lemon & Earl Grey loaf cakes 22
  swede & ginger cake 128–9
sweet potato
  pecan-studded sweet potato brownies 68–9
  spiced caramel bundt cake 106
  sticky toffee pudding with toffee sauce 97–8

T
tahini 68
tapioca flour/cornflour (cornstarch) 14, 17, 20, 59, 72, 82, 106, 112, 119, 131–2, 136
tarts
  chocolate orange tarts with Mayan spices 104–5
  fig & honey tarts 64–5
  ginger-chocolate & orange frozen tart 54–5
  pistachio & raspberry tart 62–3
  rhubarb & custard tarts 24–5
  salted caramel & chocolate tarts 114–15
  strawberry & basil tart 52–3
teff flour 31, 45–7, 90, 97–8, 119–23, 136
toffee, sticky toffee pudding with toffee sauce 97–9
tofu, lemon meringue pies 17–19
trifle, simple summer 60–1

V
vanilla
  vanilla cheesecake 32–3
  vanilla coconut frosting 96
vegetables 137
  see also specific vegetables

W
walnut 73–6, 124
  banana walnut loaf 82–3
wholemeal rye flour 84, 136
wholemeal spelt flour 73–6, 82, 136

X
xanthan gum 8, 17, 19, 22, 25, 28, 119, 130, 137

Z
zucchini see courgette

Free-From Index

DAIRY-FREE RECIPES (DF)

banana buckwheat pancakes 48–9
banana walnut loaf 82–3
beetroot red velvet cake 94–6
blueberry & lime cheesecakes 12–13
buckwheat, citrus & lavender sablés 30–1
buckwheat, hazelnut & cinnamon shorties 80–1
caramel & chocolate mini cakes 70–2
carrot, orange & pistachio cakes 50–1
chai & cashew shortbread 110–11
chai latte cheesecakes 88–9
cheesecake base recipe 131
chocolate, rye & chestnut roulade 126–7
chocolate aubergine fondant 108–9
chocolate beetroot domes 77–9
chocolate orange tarts with Mayan spices 104–5
Christmas fruit & root cake with candied fruit & glazed nuts 121–3
courgette (zucchini), gooseberry & elderflower layer cake 45–7
fig & honey tarts 64–5
ginger-chocolate & orange frozen tart 54–5
heritage carrot layer cake 73–6
hipster shortbread 84–5
lemon & Earl Grey loaf cakes 22–3
lemon meringue pies 17–19
lime, coconut & courgette (zucchini) cake 14–16
mango & passion fruit cheesecake 40–1
marquise au chocolat 86–7
olive oil & avocado mousse 58–9
orange, butternut & poppy seed loaf 28–9
passion fruit & parsnip mini cakes 34–5
pastry 130
peach, rosemary & olive oil friands 58–9
pecan-studded sweet potato brownies 68–9
pistachio & raspberry tart 62–3
pumpkin, khorasan & chai bundt cakes 100–1
quick date & pecan bread 90–1
rhubarb, strawberry & parsnip roulade 36–7
rhubarb & custard tarts 24–5
rhubarb & orange bundt cakes 20–1
rye, buckwheat & winter fruit muffins 124–5
rye cocoa-nut cookies 116–17
salted caramel & chocolate tarts 114–15
simple summer trifle 60–1
spiced blood orange & clementine cake 112–13
spiced caramel bundt cake 106–7
spiced pumpkin pies 92–3
spicy vegan chocolate cake 118–20
sticky toffee pudding with toffee sauce 97–9
strawberry & basil tart 52–3
summer berry layer cake with coconut cream 42–4
swede & ginger cake 128–9
vanilla cheesecake 32–3
vegan pastry cream 131

GLUTEN-FREE RECIPES (GF)

banana buckwheat pancakes 48–9
blueberry & lime cheesecakes 12–13
buckwheat, citrus & lavender sablés 30–1
buckwheat, hazelnut & cinnamon shorties 80–1
caramel & chocolate mini cakes 70–2
carrot, orange & pistachio cakes 50–1
chai latte cheesecakes 88–9
cheesecake base recipe 131
chocolate aubergine fondant 108–9
chocolate beetroot domes 77–9
chocolate orange tarts with Mayan spices 104–5
Christmas fruit & root cake with candied fruit & glazed nuts 121–3
courgette (zucchini), gooseberry & elderflower layer cake 45–7

custard 132
fig & honey tarts 64–5
ginger-chocolate & orange frozen
lemon & basil posset 26–7
lemon & Earl Grey loaf cakes 22–3
lemon meringue pies 17–19
lime, coconut & courgette (zucchini) cake 14–16
mango & passion fruit cheesecake 40–1
marquise au chocolat 86–7
olive oil & avocado mousse 58–9
orange, butternut & poppy seed loaf 28–9
passion fruit & parsnip mini cakes 34–5
pastry 130
peach, rosemary & olive oil friands 58–9
pecan-studded sweet potato brownies 68–9
pistachio & raspberry tart 62–3
quick date & pecan bread 90–1
rhubarb, strawberry & parsnip roulade 36–7
rhubarb & custard tarts 24–5
rhubarb & orange bundt cakes 20–1
salted caramel & chocolate tarts 114–15
simple summer trifle 60–1
spiced blood orange & clementine cake 112–13
spiced caramel bundt cake 106–7
spiced pumpkin pies 92–3
spicy vegan chocolate cake 118–20
sticky toffee pudding with toffee sauce 97–9
strawberry & basil tart 52–3
summer berry layer cake with coconut cream 42–4
vanilla cheesecake 32–3
vegan custard 132

vegan pastry cream 131

VEGAN RECIPES (VG)

banana buckwheat pancakes 48–9
banana walnut loaf 82–3
beetroot red velvet cake 94–6
blueberry & lime cheesecakes 12–13
buckwheat, citrus & lavender

sablés 30–1
buckwheat, hazelnut & cinnamon shorties 80–1
chai & cashew shortbread 110–11
chai latte cheesecakes 88–9
cheesecake base recipe 131
chocolate orange tarts with Mayan spices 104–5
fig & honey tarts 64–5
ginger-chocolate & orange frozen tart 54–5
hipster shortbread 84–5
lemon & basil posset 26–7
lemon meringue pies 17–19
mango & passion fruit cheesecake 40–1
olive oil & avocado mousse 58–9
pastry 130
pistachio & raspberry tart 62–3
pumpkin, khorasan & chai bundt cakes 100–1
rhubarb & custard tarts 24–5
rye cocoa-nut cookies 116–17
salted caramel & chocolate tarts 114–15
spiced pumpkin pies 92–3
spicy vegan chocolate cake 118–20
sticky toffee pudding with toffee sauce 97–9
strawberry & basil tart 52–3
swede & ginger cake 128–9
vanilla cheesecake 32–3
vegan custard 132
vegan meringue 17–19
vegan pastry cream 24–5, 131

WHEAT-FREE RECIPES (WF)

banana buckwheat pancakes 48–9
blueberry & lime cheesecakes 14
buckwheat, citrus & lavender sablés 30–1
buckwheat, hazelnut & cinnamon shorties 80–1
caramel & chocolate mini cakes 70–2
carrot, orange & pistachio cakes 50–1
chai latte cheesecakes 88–9
cheesecake base recipe 131
chocolate, rye & chestnut roulade 126–7
chocolate aubergine fondant 108–9

chocolate beetroot domes 77–9
chocolate orange tarts with Mayan spices 104–5
Christmas fruit & root cake with candied fruit & glazed nuts 121–3
courgette (zucchini), gooseberry & elderflower layer cake 45–7
custard 132
fig & honey tarts 64–5
ginger-chocolate & orange frozen tart 54–5
hipster shortbread 84–5
lemon & basil posset 26–7
lemon & Earl Grey loaf cakes 22–3
lemon meringue pies 17–19
lime, coconut & courgette (zucchini) cake 14–16
mango & passion fruit cheesecake 40–1
marquise au chocolat 86–7
olive oil & avocado mousse 58–9
orange, butternut & poppy seed loaf 28–9
passion fruit & parsnip mini cakes 34–5
pastry 130
peach, rosemary & olive oil friands 58–9
pecan-studded sweet potato brownies 68–9
pistachio & raspberry tart 62–3
quick date & pecan bread 90–1
rhubarb, strawberry & parsnip roulade 36–7
rhubarb & custard tarts 24–5
rhubarb & orange bundt cakes 20–1
rye, buckwheat & winter fruit muffins 124–5
rye cocoa-nut cookies 116–17
salted caramel & chocolate tarts 114–15
simple summer trifle 60–1
spiced blood orange & clementine cake 112–13
spiced caramel bundt cake 106–7
spiced pumpkin pies 92–3
spicy vegan chocolate cake 118–20
sticky toffee pudding with toffee sauce 97–9
strawberry & basil tart 52–3
summer berry layer cake with coconut cream 42–4

vanilla cheesecake 32–3
vegan custard 132
vegan pastry cream 131